DAY OCEAN STATE OF STARS' NIGHT
POEMS & WRITINGS 1989 & 1999-2006

Acknowledgements

The Tango was published as a collaboration with Scalapino's photos and with the work of artist Marina Adams by Granary Books, 2001. *It's go in/ quiet illumined grass/land* was published by The Post-Apollo Press in 2002. *'Can't' is 'Night'* was written for June Watanabe and Company for a collaboration with dancers and musicians. It was performed at the Headlands and Yerba Buena in San Francisco in 2004. Parts of *'Can't' is 'Night'* appeared in *Belladonna, Conjunctions,* and *HOW2.* Poems from "The Forest is in the Euphrates River" appeared in *The New Review, The Pip Gertrude Stein Awards for Poetry in English, Shampoo* and *Atomic Poetry;* prose from it appeared in *The Brooklyn Rail.* Poems from "DeLay Rose" appeared in *CutBank, The Recluse, Sonora Review,* and *Traffic.*

Leslie Scalapino

Day Ocean State of Stars' Night

Poems & Writings

1989 & 1999-2006

EL-E-PHANT

GREEN INTEGER
KØBENHAVN & LOS ANGELES
2007

GREEN INTEGER BOOKS
Edited by Per Bregne
København / Los Angeles

Distributed in the United States by Consortium Book
Sales and Distribution, 1045 Westgate Drive, Suite 90
Saint Paul, Minnesota 55114-1065
Distributed in England and throughout Europe by
Turnaround Publisher Services
Unit 3, Olympia Trading Estate
Coburg Road, Wood Green, London N22 6TZ
44(0)2088293009

(323) 857-1115 / http://www.greeninteger.com
Green Integer
6022 Wilshire Boulevard, Suite 200A
Los Angeles, California 90036 USA

First Green Integer Edition 2007

Design: Per Bregne
Typography: Kim Silva
Cover photograph: Leslie Scalapino
by Joan Bobkoff © 2005

LIBRARY OF CONGRESS CATALOGING IN PUBLICATION DATA
Leslie Scalapino [1947]
Day Ocean State of Stars' Night:
Poems & Writings 1989 & 1999-2006
ISBN: 978-1-933382-83-8
p. cm – An EL-E-PHANT Book
I. Title II. Series

Contents

'Can't' is 'Night'

My text is for dancers June Watanabe and Noh Master Anshin Uchida, and for improvisational musicians Pauline Oliveros, Toyoji Tomita, Shoko Hikage, and Philip Gelb. I performed in relation to the music, reading while I walked and moved with the dancers, in collaboration as June Watanabe and Company, at Yerba Buena in San Francesco in 2004.

(1)   re — separation of character and

                                                                    night.

                                    'no language' 'with it' — movement or language, here

(2)   the real-time event (occurring) is the only thing there is/ *'was'*
                                 they've destroyed language so we have to destroy it in it not
                                                                    movement

                                    night exists at day — but is not the same night so

                                    night is not-existing *then then* is open to the senses

                    she (someone) says our language is to remove boundless character of

                                                                    night,

          that's terror.   when?

          their 'lie' — as that one's

                        is to substitute for night, hers night 'terror' — say how ____ .to

                        reverse *'their'* reverse of the boundless character of night can't be

                                                                    said

                                                           or moved either

          even though outside

                        blues can't exist outside either — as separation of character and

                                                                    night.

                                         so it's separation of character and night 2

(3)   our prisoner

was found on the ground outside standing before Bagram U.S.

military prison in Afghanistan which we've decimated, lie to, for

something they didn't do —

the US military   take him in

beat him to death, prisoners who interrogated chained hang while

'our' marines beat them to keep them

awake if they fall asleep when hanging there

present —blues can't exist outside — or in character

no night being — as woman who

says 'our' language is to reverse

night's

being — without edge — any night

terror

he'd committed no crime standing outside might

be

terrorist

her separation of 'our' language from any real-

time night

order

(4)   Major Elizabeth Rouse, pathologist, checked the homicide box

              to say he was murdered by US military —events don't fit

              in, at all — aren't in language either — Major Elizabeth Rouse

                                               told the truth

                                 blues can't exist outside now for

                    night is not-existing *then then* is open to the senses to

              newspapers say (their corpses) one Iraqi man walks

                                      forward holds his AK47

              above his head, he defies our huge army somehow to walk to it

              what's he thinking? as our soldiers kill him in movement he

                                               can't do

(5)   says

                          after the person's attack on one in his

                          saying one's motion — is fixed, fixing it — where its

                                                            intent

                          is to have no place its motion is its theory

                                                               he

says the motion is one's fixed self, which, if one speaks, one

he says *'imagines'* attack of his

on one, that *is*

that (*is* his reverse of one and others)

he says one is self-centered in seeing it — not one is seeing his

actions outside in fact — so, there is no event, no real-time

— at all in that their/his language changes it always — is then

'only'

not its past action — or occurrence *now*

separation of thinking and being

the same is occurring outside *'from'* war they make saying to them

it's liberating them not attacking

before, our language is only coercion, in every conversation reverse

event — any except

themselves in *'our'* language

— in space at all — language is then

(6)   since

an event's — not language — separation of character

                                                                    and

night — is outside movement's — separation of character and

                                                            night 2

day. as. bud 'dis-placing' is

        lineage. — both. (both the bud and 'dis-placing') single is 'tree's'

                                                        buds

                                                        there

        day. "we dropped a few civilians, but what do you do?" the sniper
        says "1 Iraqi soldier and 25 women and children, I didn't take the
                                                        shot,

                but 1 Iraqi soldier standing among 2 or 3 civilians,"

                sharp-shooter Sergeant Schrumpf remembering the

                woman going down — "the chick was in the way"

        events are against movement   can't be in

        one's movement

        'dis-placing' terror by killing. not movement dis-placing language

                        the Kurds just move in that space

                waves on a line across it ('we've') courted to fight and

                dropped them to be, were, slaughtered again court

to have them attack on the lands

where they're slaughtered then wave on lines on one side in

space 'we'

label them freedom fighters on the line's other side the same

ones 'we' label terror

ists

as words labels space—one— is there difference between the

'basic space of

phenomena'

phrase

and

the space of planets

moon

outside

movement?

(7)   "I expected them to surrender I thought they would all capitulate."

in the 3 days that followed,

they did not. — many of the Iraqis, Sergeant Redmond

said, attacked headlong into the cutting fire of tanks

and Bradley fighting vehicles

"I wouldn't call it bravery," he

said. "I'd call it stupidity. we value a
soldier's life so much more than they
do. an AK47 isn't going to do
nothing against a Bradley"
since we're to reverse with 'our' language — boundless

characteristic of night

as   day order

Iraqis are fighting   tanks, aircraft, artillery, prison camps, torture

Sergeant Redmond thinks that's stupid. for him relation

of language to movement: is

none?

the relation of language to movement is: 'none' in order to make

that   relation — *there*

the only chance they have is

at all

night

14

(8)   the phrase

'the basic space of phenomena' is different from night space?

night's in

event is 'the basic space of phenomena' before occurrence

of the phenomena

'we're' 'our'

language is to reverse the boundless characteristic of night,

she (someone) says,   to reverse night's

night is everywhere fierce fighting in Kut the south where

desperate

Iraqis armed with rifles charged tanks in suicide

raid. 'we'

mowed them down

says Lt. Col. B.P. McCoy — tracer rounds   lit night

sky

there

the battalion arrived after dark and settled

down for the night

night is in the newspaper page only

(9)   with no

                                                                      warning shot, fire killing
                                 family of fifteen — or they fight *our* tanks with AK47s
                          from pick-up trucks 'ours' say those others are only lied to, not

brave   in 'our' movement

(10)   there is no way ('reason') to live, following the day. I thought.

                                                                 our language is to (she says) reverse —

                          the 'basic space of phenomena' (phrase) and the space of planets moon's

                                                                                           not outside

(11)   he characterizes 'our' enemy, Iraqis, as murderers,

                                                                 cowards, thugs — and he praises the US force

                          for their kindness and goodness.   their Iraqi bodies lay

                          along the road. living these are all across night, they cross night, are

                                                                                                    not

                                                                                                    its

                                                                                           character

                                                                                 to reverse trees

                          marines came and Iraqis left so quickly left cooking fires alight

`   and their guns they need them

Baghdad plunges into darkness   —   can't *be*.

           'our' war everywhere — isn't/is — in 'our' language

                                      in movement of

                                            one

(12)   has made living impossible. any way. 'they'

                                            destroy

                                   language. destroy

                                          night

                              fight with your hands

              they exhorted   the Iraqi people

              the Kurds just move in that space

        waves on a line across it ('we've') courted to fight and

        dropped them to be, were, slaughtered again

'we' have nowhere ahead — either —any way.

                    she says 'our' language is to reverse the bound

                              less characteristic of night

                                            to

        destroy night to — without language — in it — two— outside

                                                                    17

(13)

destroy that language

for that

night

there

(14) this isn't about suffering we'd be suffering if 'we' *were*

happy

she (someone) says 'our' language is reverse of the bound

less that's terrorist

terror characteristic of night's everything

in my language / is 'ours' only — to enter the boundless

night

night's

without language any

basic space of phenomena's not outside or in — is it *there*

also?

a man (someone) says a (this) syntax is a state of being

insanity — but it's attention only — to itself

I thought attention, and as its subject, cannot be insane? or

may be breaking 'his' reason this   now phenomena

'our' being 'happy' (emotion that's convention) is 'ours'

not

in events outside is insane

the outside and the inside cannot be *there*

in 'our' character? if it is uncompounded

or re — in attention (one cannot be regarding), either —

that

separation of character and

night

night cannot be seen

regarding is separation of one from others   only

here   not-regarding

collective now — having driven the Iraqis insane

attention now is insane — is dependent on the separation

of character and night 2, not in movement— either — them

in 'our' thought, language, 'our' movement is before

(language) and later.

the civilians had to be killed on the road

fleeing Baghdad because they were there as

'we're' (invading)

— is not 'our' movement in that it has occurred already —

(15)   the breaking of reason not inside movement of

one's

—   moon and movement — of one's or

at all (and moon) — is the breaking of reason.

one's is 'theirs'

(16)

it's 'not repeated' — 'to produce' —that is:

'be-dualistic' — at all

is   night's space

even —   not

their — that's outside — despair is one's physical

movement bud's

lineage

outside

at once

on one night

(17)

to reverse

'our' language's reverse of nights night-boundless-

ness   or movement

of/in

one's — disintegrating also —

skin that's movement only   *then*

'can't'

is

'night'

21

(18)   their despair is one's physical movement (not).

                                                    language is

                                                    crushed.

                    "2   Iraqis sat in despair." after their dead

                                        coincide with night after

                    (and after night's over). the breaking of reason — a

                                                    man seeing.

(19)   as if by favoring war

                                                    is meant its reverse

                                                    reverse trees

                                                    (that are)

                                                    night characteristic

                    I can't see/comprehend it's (before night) 'the basic

                                                    space of phenomena'

                    phrase

                    he's been reversed in language — 'we're' 'killing as its

                                                    reverse'

                    'our' character is even in night_____ say how?

(20)   the breaking of reason

                    is silent seeing   movement (of one's)

                    language

since these 're in utter isolation only,   that is

everyone

                                                                is

as language   as social/*and* dawn.

their despair is one's physical movement (not).

(21)   long movement (single)   does not repeat

                                        the outside

'isn't'/ 'is' the same as 'his' night crushing language

                                        of one — night's

                                                space even?

                                he/someone else intends actual

                sky even to reverse its night/as language/one not —

                while (one) dawn-waking actually ('at' dawn *yet* one *there*

                                                also)

                                        dawn in the same space

as one   is.

someone/it's not possible for him to do any thing even

    without attacking someone else first,   *he can't,*

he's never done so.   defensive

                                       is

be-dualistic

he can't stand (in front of others) without first

                    attacking someone what is

this space   (in front of others)?

    he can't sustain

    others because he

       will not.   *'then'*

                        present.

   isn't reason — reason is insane

                  movement of one's

             is theirs

                    their despair

already   it?

that space/social even and not dualistic isn't

  even

                                    because that would be dualistic,
              it   night sky *would*.   'be-dualistic'

                                          in   nights not mirror

              and: 'our' tyrant makes/'is' the war expanding in

              an outside the outside breaking reason

      is —

              'isn't'/ 'is' — the same as 'his' night crushing language
                                                    of one — night's

      space even.   long movement (single)

              sky even to reverse its night/as language/'one not' —

                                    while (one) dawn-waking actually ('at'

                              dawn *yet* one *there* dawn also

      (22)   A wave is sucked into sleep then

              the forest is completely separate from the

              people always —   outside and

                                          separate from the war

                                                    though

              the forest destroyed or growing

is in the war

the forest is balanced on the night and

then balanced on the day

at the same time. after — is the same time later

the forest wave if the trees

are still even on night

is one wave moving on day

that's war whether day

appears still. day is in war. separate from the forest

day still appears. the forest

is black at night black

fire goes away at night though night's still

the dark gangly sleek moose come out and shy

away

vertically

though one moves

across night for long distances wave of

forest

(23)   immense light on the endless lake at

                                                        night black

                         the ducks fly across it

                                                        night vertically

                         the dark gangly sleek moose roam at

                                                        will in the forest

                         wave on the endless still lake

                                                        never black

                                                        then

                                        the endless lake moves night

                                                        black

(24)   the forest rushes to the road

                                                        push

                         steel rumpled thunderous clouds are

                                                        at the road at

                         the forest meeting ahead — at one's side

                         forest wave rushing horizontally

                                                        to

the rumpled steel clouds everywhere ver-

tically

race to the endless lake steel light in it

sky of rain descends everywhere vertically

then

black bear rambles gracefully in the sheets

rain-vertical-grass

in day separating night horizontally

above

(25)   occurrence in structure unseen

words on a sign "owl rafting" the

dark mist separates morning from night so the

forest wave

begins

to rush

but the forest moved at night

unseen by one rafting

the night rafting the owl, unseen by one, the

forest rafting

                                the owl

        rafting the night forest — one rafting

only   and unseen owl-night

at   forest-wave

                        there

(26)   — woman saying our language is to reverse

night — is 'for' that — not producing —

night uncontrolled

is occurrence in structure unseen

at all

not producing at all — one's seeing —

but the forest moved

at

night rafting

The Tango

"Astor Piazzola was writing [composing, in his tangos]
the struggle of modern life." Eduardo Smisson

The text's internal debate is the author's 'comparison'
of her mind phenomena to exterior phenomena, laying these
alongside each other 'actually' — such as the mind's comparison
to dawn, to magnolias, to color of night, as if these are manifes-
tations of mind phenomena, which they are *here*.

Placing one's mind-actions beside magnolias (words).

'The same figure repeated everywhere,' a line or passage may recur
exactly as slipping out of, returning, slipping out of, a frame of concentration
and sound.

What's place — war in 'night'

      pink roses — aren't the pink sun rising — are 'social'
only? both

      "night" on famine — as one — real-time

      (walking in garbage it wasn't night) — not in time
either
      'night' 'night' 'won't ever dis-place it' — it can dis-
place it — where it occurs

_____

      he doesn't trust one because it's one — observation
('so' present-time) of a real-time event (past) — to make
these be the same 'in order' to dis-place 'them' and one

_____

      "famine" "famine" is 'to be' impermanence — not
formed event. 'as' quoted event, i.e. seen. — first — early,
when one is a child — there

_____

      "emotion is not the cause of impermanence." *is* it?
I've thought it causes. not the cause of events' occurrence
(there) *as* impermanence

_____

first seeing the ship or seeing the man dying? — the
ship on the ocean, heavy weighed water — black waves at
dock of "famine" "famine" is emotion adjacent to
observation — unfixed.
or it is the observation/the first real-time event itself
(famine) there? one will not be event.

———————

not 'seeing' on 'nature' — or on the mind itself either
— between these? — not between these

neither — yet 'attention' — space? not past.

———————

pink roses — aren't the pink sun rising — are 'social'
only? both

"night" on famine — as one — real-time

(walking in garbage it wasn't night) — not in time
either

'night' 'night' 'won't ever dis-place it' — it can dis-
place it — where it occurs

— to make these be the same 'in order' to dis-place
'them' and one

'in order' — in spring, later — both.
as it not being first, but at the same time.

———————

34

yet to mute one's ego — which is in order for that
ground to *be* there

'in order' — in spring, later — both.
as it not being first, occurrence at all, but at the same
time.

———————

weight 'follows' — this 'a' night occurs — 'not the
same thing as' — 'on the same level' — is not following
ever? — 'night' is first to it.

what's place — war in 'night' — which is occurring
now

———————

'at all' is social — *is* blossoming trees *or* when one's
outside there (so there's moon *there*) as outside is the only
existing — both

———————

a man walks up to one out of the blue — before
unknown — and says one's paranoid in the context. — one
viewing real-time past event of a man starving holding out
his cup lying in garbage as 'its location only' — where 'one
self not existing now' walked — from a ship docked there —
the
man walking to one because only the relation in space given
— in that, if the 'meaning' of the event is given (or even
placement as being *what's occurring* —
that frames occurrence) that is not to dis-locate it,
would be formed event only.
which is what event *is* (that it's already)
it is not being an 'event' there even — at all — to *be*
only relational — to 'have it be' that — then the later man
walking to one in some other [instance]
is 'that' magnolia bud. both. but not that of the earlier
event even.

———————

35

is black water 'social' *only?* — in that, if the 'meaning'
of the event is given (or placement as *what's occurring* —
even that frames occurrence)

there is no 'social' *there*
it's *only* social — same with black water — place black
water to be social — yet it *is*

pink rose — completely unrelated — pink sun rose or
set? in fact.

───────

placement in space — is oneself — only? and — moon
— rose

───────

it is not even to state location in a different way, it is
not to re-state conditions even. (those conditions are not the
ground even.)

the man strolling to one (years ago — 'so' in time) —
saying that altering of ground itself — to *be* impermanence,
to have it be that — that 'relational only' is "paranoid" — ?
— this is beside the point. that would be to say only one saw
it, it is not there — he reorders intention — to 'fix' location
'as' social?

him not doing that 'intentionally' — isn't? — there
occurs location's relation first

───────

everyone — to be — the man strolling to one —
being *not* dependent

───────

to change *location's relation* to construction of meaning — that one would not reproduce construction of self as context, in that, *ground itself is altered first* and occurs as only relational

conversely, by time being abandoned — it is not based in time — the man holding out his cup not caring, because he's dying, once seen lying in garbage, by being in the writing's placement as relational location, is not relegated to time (is not 'in memory' only)

it is not even to state location in a different way, it is *not* to re-state conditions even. (those conditions are not the ground even.)

———————

not the day being within the blossom

as in reverse (rather than the *day* in it) — the blossom
isn't in the *day* either

'not a black dawn/a black dawn' is real-time only.
_____

wants to see — 'authority' — of 'other' men — from
one, that one would be of only 'them'
there being only 'them' 'so' he is subjunctive

'not a black dawn/a black dawn' is real-time only.
_____

beggars whirling in dust fighting

whirling beggars fighting in the dust — while the
high rugged brown mountain crags are still, a day-moon is
lying on a high brown jutting mountain top. the day-moon
and mountain's separation (while the moon is lying on
mountain's top) in the high fawn-brown blue atmosphere

is [that] [people's joy]?

a day-moon at the same time as a brown high
mountain — their separation

the day-moon lying on the mountain — their
separation — it's on high altitude jagged crag desert.

———————————

military wolves — still shoot the people in a stone-
fenced corral open on a brown mountain and bury the
corpses in a shallow grave until the families come to pay the
army to retrieve them for burial.

military wolves

———————————

the day-moon and mountain's separation — (while
moon is on mountain's rim) —military wolves

subjectivity/not-and /language 'as' black dawn *only*

then (when alive). — (subjunctive.) — black dawn
isn't? — so it has to pass. both.

subordinate nothing black trees-ocean night

magnolia buds —that haven't opened—
subjectivity/language *only* — both

subjectivity/not-and/language 'as' black dawn *only*
— *and* the man there is in anger, 'really.'
he consumes 'forward'
_____

is subjunctive — the man starving dying lying in garbage? — there not being black dawn — ?

no. not anyway — that is, anywhere. — or: subjunctive is *only* 'social.' both.

then (when alive). — (subjunctive.) — black dawn isn't? — so it has to pass. both.

——————

to ignore one's shape/events 'so' it goes on wildly — *and* — anyway.

magnolia buds — that haven't opened — subjectivity/language *only* — both.

words 'black dawn' as shape (instance that has no 'other' occurrence) which is 'their shape/and their *conceptual* shape.'

to subordinate magnolia buds — that is real-time — both.

——————

'not' for there to be 'magnolia bud (not-opened)' —

bud 'dis-placing' is lineage — both. single is 'tree's
buds there' (as *only* one's 'social' — at the same time.

a given in space — dis-place blossoming trees.
———————

people's behavior being blossoming trees — *per se*
(just as that) — and the action of it (their 'behavior') in the
trees blossoming prior — which is separate, sole

bound as 'split' (one's) 'to' conception of change as, or
in, behavior —
that was not when a child
rather than in blossoming trees — everywhere as ground
is an ocean here

so 'split' is *that* only — ocean 'in' blossoming trees —
'in fact' has to be to change people's behavior/one's as sole

in fact — itself — isn't *then*. change in blossoming
trees occurring prior to (trees). (then blossoming trees being
'social' only.)
—————

the moon is socially-based as emotion is — so it would
be itself.

a given in space — dis-place blossoming trees.
—————

'on' experience— so one's 'isn't,' is obliterated — by the referring. place this to: seeing 'at all' is social — *is* blossoming trees

      or when one's outside there (so there's moon *there*) — as outside is the only existing — both

      ———————

      'seeing' the man starving lying in garbage — yet to conceptually place the site only in relation in space (to foreground and background, or future, simply) — to buildings — is *not* to iterate those as conditions, present
      his dying is to be *not* in relation to space, or to conjecture

      it's *not* to be that

      'as' 'blossoming trees' are one's subjectivity/language 'there' —

      ———————

just oneself being roses only

roses only — people in speaking or in their limbs —
being that — to each other also

_____

bound as 'split' (one's) 'to' conception of change as, or
in, behavior —
that was not when a child
so 'split' is *that* only — ocean 'in' blossoming trees —
'in fact' has to be to change people's behavior/one's as sole

What's place —'moon' 'rose'

     Before, saw dog's end back crushed from hurtling car.
its head curled to see walks anyway from greenery — here
the men's delicate backs' cages move the present only
     as if there were sleeping, but the backs move
     'emerge' is on one level the men's backs curling or
straightening.

        —————

     the men's delicate backs' cages move the light that's
'at' present — before, the broken dog's crushed end the back
that's curled to see still walking
     their
     on curling straightening backs move *that* light

        —————

     one's emotion itself volatile event is not 'initiating'
one's dying and living? — nor is one's seeing?
     their own hands move them on the same level in the
light, they're lying in the light

     the men's curled backs lying beside their hands move
them. no one having memory ever (only constructing concept
— concept as motion —of that) and dog's crushed back then
seeing as the head skitters to road's edge
     there
     is seeing outside itself

        —————

'friends' 'is' convention only (or 'custom' isn't
initiating one's 'dying and living'?) — and their backs lying
move the present only
the backs move the light in that they're lying on the
same level

———————

people's emotions are not 'there being outside events'
— nor is there 'no relation' to events outside their
apprehension even

there aren't going to be 'friends'— one's prior concept

the men's backs move only the light

———————

— which is —there not in hurtling road

they're lying and their hands move on that same
level—the men are 'only' their backs — if so 'there are not
backs'
one's hands lie in air too —(and have no 'back' there)

———————

to have that view
it is not necessary. backs

military wolves rose

———————

— who have one be only convention —
only if one notices? —
others aren't convention? while these men's backs
move the light

————

the relation between emotion and event, neither
causing the other. nor do they have no relation. people
submitted — as customary functions — to a friend — in their
view — and they're —
only *social* — motions for the other

———————

not erase excruciating pain in some
social gesture of repression
in one
it is not *out of body*

———————

white orchids are 'by' persimmons — causal,
disrupting. — so 'seeing' itself is opposing streaming. —
white orchids dependent there on persimmons is social *only*.
— *are* social only (both)

is in any case created

———————

crushed back the head sees skittering walks — from
hurtling road, greenery
friends as 'that,' i.e. not existing. are *social. is social.*

— their back cage's move it, is the light-and-
language? both.
but the men moving there didn't speak. may.

———————

if there
no 'friends' (as *everyone isn't* that) — nothing social —
only being child until dying

delicate back dies sometime. — but these men's backs
move light here only

———————

only being child until dying — everyone — is their
delicate back dies sometime
theirs one

— is 'basis' — standing or curling? only

———————

moving is floating ears — elephants — a trunk and
face floating on one's ears
either charging or floating on grass, at once
man's chest: as trunk floating on ears of elephant's —
he's that, coming. ears on 'trunk recoiled or forward.'

———————

his dying is to be *not* in relation to
space, or to conjecture

_____

some are

standing or curling. rose — is not — rose (they rose).
both.
subjectivity/language is — the delicate food system
disturbed famine reappears —?
were killed practicing in the monasteries — shipped
to labor, dying, trains shipping them, ringed in by barbed
wire haul on dam sites tunnels exhaustion famine in lines.
the same figure repeated everywhere changes it there as if
changed but not either from within or without that

_____

if the back's constructed — and moves the light — is
subjectivity/language *only* — they're not 'speaking'
that is 'speaking' — social — both

subjectivity/language constructed *also* and those men
move the light — so —
social isn't *anything?* — there — walking — either

_____

moon rose — that is —appears to
moon rose
on or resting on mountain's top — edge
horizon —
men's delicate backs standing move — is separate —
from them
there at all — both

_____

there is no basis of the blossoming   —one's subjectivity/language—
tree—there—   him lying starving in the street—or
                                                       crossing the street—is?

          and is 'as' one's
subjectivity/language—'there'   'the blossoming trees'

          _____   black trees then?

                                                       _____

                    future — movement
                    is 'not' night — or
                    'in' 'night' — either yet
                    ahead — so there are not functions ever

                    _____

                    the men standing and curling while the backs lying.
          — in the place.
                    social — (is 'getting along with' people only?) or one
          "doesn't get along with people"— is functions only (someone
          makes that occur — by ostracism —
                    one has no function then)

                    _____

the man has kindness — *is* standing lying — or at
night curling
where
one holds his back

at *'night'* — ?

———————

must 'accept' death of others. — except them. except
him. (can't) is them him *also.*

at *'night' any night* is *can't*

———————

the day-moon and mountain's   military wolves
separation (while moon is on mountain's
top) in the high brown blue atmosphere   place black water to be trees-ocean

———————

day. moon. rose. — is on a mountain — is one's own
back — is *any night* — (isn't the same as night)

is *can't.* their separation is there.

———————

the flesh is not asleep while one's sleeping. at *any*
time? — no difference between 'apprehension' —
it's the *same* in one?
— blossoming trees — outside — or 'there not being
memory at all' if the flesh is not asleep ever

or that's rest as *not* sleeping
the relation between 'no memory occurring' ever
(only constructing — thought as motion — in anyone —)

and the flesh not asleep ever (even while one's
sleeping) — is blossoming trees 'outside', that is *also*

————

the relation between the dog's crushed back and its
seeing
apprehension isn't by itself even. both.

crushed isn't by itself — either skittering from side of
hurtling car on flimsy countryside

————

some friend wanted faceless mother slaves. whatever for?

not to speak, is *social* as people being functions? they 'think' it is — not to see people's faces —there — is *no inclination* on their part.

   — duty — is nothing — no functions as one. both.
   is wasting —wanting — speaking — social

one's subjectivity/language *is* one's back's motion

———————

he says — one suffering as *is* inferior *then* (free of suffering being itself bliss, i.e. 'indication' that one is free) and 'that one is free'

people's feelings, one's suffering, is there wild. moon rose and is people's feelings wild
   one's suffering, one's kindness — *is* 'isn't the same as night'

————

hemmed in streaming — being attacked — as
conception *also* —
others streaming being attacked — all over the place
— she says 'it's never happened to *her*'
isn't hemmed in streaming walking — there is no
'outside' — ?

she's so protected — 'it's never happened to *her*' —
and it's everywhere — there's no place. —

———————

as their sense that 'the flesh itself isn't anything' as
opposing others et al

then it's only one — in their 'social' realm — neither,
as there's no memory et al — and the flesh's 'memory of
being free' 'as' 'there'

———————

— one's subjectivity/language is their or one's motion
only there?

seeing being only a motion even (in walking, say)

one has no back — yet. — not even 'in' 'night' —
not even past movements' 'night' — either — and is
future 'nights'
where(?) no movement of one's occurs — future is
same as one's motions without extension *now*

one's motion ahead — is only one *now* —nights rose

———————

to find something out — one's motions without
extension in this place — not even — past movements'
extension *now* — either — nights rose.

forward into a motion where?
subjectivity/language constructed *also* and moves the
light — so — social isn't *'anything'*? — there. — walking —
either

———————

leafy layers leaves as above and below, a floor and
sky, walking, lit, out, the horizontal

subjectivity/language is one's back's motion. there.
both.

———————

he's walking — hemmed in streaming — being
attacked

in the flesh not ever being asleep while (one's)
sleeping — hemmed in streaming — *also*

at *'night' any night* is *can't* — he's/one's 'outside' in it
— *both*

The Tango —'night' any night is can't

(Astor Piazzola's tangos: the tango is relentless. The embrace
— a couple? — entwining goes and goes. It skips, jumps
ahead of a horizon — itself — resuming. The tango is a
hopscotch 'ahead' of them, a couple, it's for convenience of
maneuver, it's for intense love.)

separation the *that's,* outside as *same* the interior only
(separation) that's —. separation a to illumines

'live why?' — one some on dependent — illumines — no
place

—————

and then — if there *were* that — there's 'no night' either

—————

as if from 'their' conception/ view there were only 'that'
'one' — and only 'that' 'one' and only 'that' 'one' — an
interior — and 'that' 'one' in it

except no interior in 'their' view (*as* 'that' 'one' and 'that'
'one' only structure)

—————

though cold and dead, 'social dominance' is a part —
the tango goes in and in to it

and that were 'social' dominance as what there is only
— or it were *not* structure even — and *no* interior

—————

elephants' ears floating in grass. — recoiled or forward trunk. — moves. — on ears lying in air. — trunk as man's chest. — coming. — 'there'.

it is never isolated

---

my

conception of 'directly initiate thought/emotion' 'at' other's thought-constructions —so that they *are* the same time —

so as not to have that social order they are or make outside and they 'are' streams in oneself opposing each other only, at one instant in one.

(one's not knowing — inexperienced or not seeing) and one's 'knowing' as that which leads — are together so something occurs that 'was' neither

dying itself is 'any night is can't' — and — in that blossoming trees — even as 'aren't that' (in fall) — are other than oneself — *are* one's 'not knowing' also

blossoming trees are 'opposing only' 'in' a place.

---

the formation even some one's thought 'makes'
(running on itself or 'to run it on' itself in some other
thought (of one's), at that instant [of itself]) — such as: at the
same instant, as some one's thought, a man deigns to look at
only some one in a group of people speaking —

any speaking only 'that' (instant) imposed — in some
one's hearing also — *night* can't exist *either* as once

————

'outside' is opposing as streaming itself — but not
disturbed?

one's feeling as happiness 'can't withstand' night? —
as not a negative space — there isn't any

————

night and 'not based in sense' — haven't been (as:)
outside of these — states of night, being — as: 'aren't' 'these'
continually

is that ground — 'night' *and* '*its* not based in sense'

and 'night' isn't the same as 'that' time (isn't the same
as itself)

————

events — as say his 'consenting to look' or night —
can't withstand — any. so opposing as streaming against
each event in the future or present —

————

one's 'not knowing' (inexperienced or not seeing) —
as: blossoming trees — either when these 'aren't' (in fall) —
or 'are' then. both.

— yet when one's faculty of 'not knowing'— such as
in being young (or also being old) — is also a state of
suffering

and takes apart

———————

him having nothing given from the other man dies?
— isn't social only. is outside. imbalanced leads night —
infuriated opposing collapsing places it? is social only

place outside — 'to place outside' — is only one's
subjectivity/language? as that — outside as conflict 'as' one
— *is* one's subjectivity/language — *only?* then?

collapsing places — yet —. *only*

'reverse directly' is 'opposing as streaming' social
only?

———————

his subjectivity luminous to one's opposing as
streaming outside — being 'outside motions' *is* —

if some one from within (is opposing directly) their
own 'subjectivity' and outside at once

in his consenting to look at only one, as that being
hierarchy as such

white orchid's interior social only? yet 'behavior' that
is 'theirs'

there would not be place that is withstanding it — the
separate motions opposed to each other as *this only*

----

a man 'consenting to look' at only one, in a group of
people — minute seeing — others (elsewhere) shipped to
labor camps, where starved — 'has' hierarchy — as
'luminosity'

single quotes ('   ') being the subjunctive — and
what is outside are together

----

she says the entire thing is 'theirs' — as if others there
were fake — in relation to 'fake' social luminosity

controls 'as' people 'seen' 'as' white orchids and
their/one not disturbed? both. ('both' is opposing-
streaming)

----

rode back in on horses raids into their own land —
and were defeated — by modern military that had invaded
grinding them, sent to camps, starved, were executed

he says that mind opposing continually is "insane"
as 'simply' not 'in' fixed or continuing social state — which
there *isn't* — but is conceptualized (and he conceptualizes
it) as shared, *isn't* — either, as the mind *per se* is opposing
fixed state continually
individual motions are dependent — orchids and
one's mind streaming-opposing

———————

the fabric of their logic (itself hierarchy) is a 'whole,'
which they say is
'analysis.' — one's 'analysis' of their 'whole' fabric,
they say is a 'whole'
(in order to dismiss it) or they say is "insane" *but it
can't be both* probably
convention of perception — can't be both 'whole' and
'insane' — unless it's theirs (they construct)

they exclude outside

———————

the tango is dependent — it disrupts — it goes in and in to outside

their logic itself hierarchy which they call 'analysis' is invisible to them —

that is not 'analysis' — because it is 'whole' — merely excluding 'outside'

_____

must 'accept' death of others. — except them. except him. (can't) is them him also.

at *'night' any night* is *can't*

_____

the flesh's 'memory of pain' and also 'memory of pleasure' — and 'memory of being free' 'there'

their 'social' realm also extended out there — their 'seeing' observation opposing and streaming as 'not there' in the sense of 'conflict only' — may be —

_____

why does one wish to frighten oneself? — at *'night'* *any night* is *can't*
dying isn't 'that' (its same) time — and — in that blossoming trees —which aren't (in fall) — are one's 'no knowing' *also*

_____

ears are as if lips — *but ears 'are' lips.* trunk as man's chest. woman's ears lying back as she lies down. forward trunk floating or lying on ears
people charging make interior motion 'outside'

_____

A child says that's because it's the nerve's 'memory of pain' not the cause being there (later, after the nerve being freed, in the pain that's *there* still)

and the flesh's 'memory of pain' and also 'memory of pleasure' — and the flesh's 'memory of being free' that's in it *only* there *are* occurring

———————

observation is its occurrence in one (at all) (also)

is subjunctive — the man starving dying lying in garbage? — there not being black dawn — ?

no. not anyway — that is, anywhere. — or: subjunctive is *only* 'social.' both.

then (when alive). — (subjunctive.) — black dawn isn't? — so it has to pass. both.

———————

motion is forward without one. either sleeping or walking, which are the same.

ears. a recoiled or forward trunk is floating on the ears.

a man's trunk, coming.

a man is the tango. is relentless.

gentleness. it is *speaking* — *there*. repeats 'just' space.

———————

the man looking at only one in a group willing his hierarchy — is making their 'insane' realm opposing, where they are

as their sense that 'the flesh itself isn't anything' as opposing others et al

then it's only one — in their 'social' realm — neither as there's no memory et al — and the flesh's 'memory of being free' 'as' 'there' — no *memory 'in' night*

———————

repeats 'just' space

their 'social' realm also extended out there — one's motion without extension in this place forward 'as' *at 'night' any night is can't* and at 'night' 'night rose' — is not the same

one's motion forward — not even there — is at *'night' any night* is *can't* — not the flesh's 'memory of being free' either — 'out there'

———————

he escapes — walks out. from his invaded land, where is hemmed in, imprisoned. lied to. now boy to lead controlled so as not to learn
military wolves
walks. then transported by trucks
'everyone is suffering' transported on trucks
mountains-high 'outside' can't change one's behavior. sole. not anyway — that is, anywhere — 'moon' 'rose' subjunctive is *only* 'social.' he escapes
is near bare moon that's in the day 'accept (the fact of) dying' sole? (or living. at all)

It's go in

quiet illumined grass

land

silver half freezing in day
                              elation the
                              outside
of the outside sky walking
                              rose

silver half freezing in day
                              moon's elation
of the outside rose, his seeing
                              on both
                              'sides'
seeing someone else at all and the
                              half freezing
elation of the outside so that's even
                              with one
continually over and over one/person

                              he will
also now person dying? is not
                              compared to
space they're in outside silver freezing
                              half
moon day now both walking rose
                              instant
running — wall — wall

someone coming to see me, he says
while
lying down
I turned
to see them, tend to them
and broke my back and now I'm
stuck
here
but doesn't have to look at or flip about
here

quiet grass land silver and
the
half brown fur mound
half
mountain
hawks fly beside it can't be
here
space
in there in that they're at the
same
time

Standing — wall — wall
    rose

    and — rose flowers, social — both

      conceptually as of dropping (being — or a view) in
space — as dropping 'out' — is not using language, here
either (?) —. slow
(which is 'one walking so slow that outraces eludes them'

to walk so slowly as not to be there with them at all

who 'are social only') — or 'outracing' 'them' ahead. neither
      yet one sight at a time — 'retains' — (a sight itself
'retains'? outside)
      and sight is only separate from language or
movement —

      as dropping out low vertical — night is both, with
no people
      but images seen at once, left there, *no seeing either*

      is wild moon? in day

      a left there — as 'left leg' — the viewer is in a separate
place from what they see (at the moment) always — the
viewer is 'they',
both

      running — wall is space —

Living in the subjunctive, social — both — is space —
it's fear propelled — isn't in one (who's in it)
or 'when it's *in* one', may be isn't *in* the others —
existing
there — seeing it in oneself only (as: not coming 'from' them,
but in one 'only' 'then' — is then freely
the relation of suffering et al to space — so it isn't in
black night)

this other sees fear coming 'from' others only — 'there'

so acts as fear in her — which is to become or hurt
them (she's)
is black night subjunctive, no, there

there's only that (one's/their) behavior in relation to
space

'Interpreted everyone' — is 'turned to be' 'one' 'only'
— (as) to rush up and there is nothing but that 'one's
fragile
in relation to them' only — said to be the occurrence then.

different from:
to rush up to them and instant is only one's, such as fear,
not *from*
them. — 'there is not' 'lineage' 'social' 'outside' 'there'
—
or 'night'
can't be
in
night

yet people on the street seen at the waist — walking
slowly, a bus moves in its middle

it's not relying on any thing even its sound there
though it is its sound 'only'? — why, its sound is not
the sight?

'they're' existing only constructed — just 'social only'
are themselves —can't see behavior-evening, either —
these are the same

I *can't see*
at all. — *is* that occurrence. *both*
Failed to see that a person in the past is what they *are*
doing, are. and they *aren't* that then and now (both)
so I didn't learn, am outside.
So seeing is space. Then *anything* occurs.

Oppression is the social space

then
someone else in the social space — 'goes for' 'to' —
perceive what's occurring

the outside isn't fear — *then* it isn't — she 'goes for' the
separation of seeing and being *as* it's occurring, its occurrence
elation
the separation of sight and language *there* — the first
time of the social space

is 'between' 'sky' (sky) — at all — daily — evening
times

indentation in space

                      a

    single
    friend's ferocity
    and
    (somewhere else — unrelated)
    crowds killing — pressed
             inside one
    to be even
             in 'space'
    that's outside

    with one (in) early evening

    freezing red leaves sea early one

    Separation of space sky rung
             O
  sun there that is outside and outside
               itself
             one's
  walking rose only and there outside
            rose O
  at side of sky on its vertical space
           separates

comparing the mind to magnolias
or to sky, because one sees.
but comparing people's actions to sky
or to war to moon outside? is in that space
then.
apprehend
behavior-evening — ferocity even
from just one — where there was no reason
bewildering — doesn't seem
'bewildering' if it's huge in multitude.
indentation so that they're even
one to evening — is no behavior-evening
any event a random space

as — did he say to her — to be silent
—that it would go away — it will never go away
as silence is an action which is the same thing

wild suffering

(so it can't go away) (so the latter is
determinacy) — not 'go away' the same thing-one

modifies
'sky' is subjunctive that's space?

white moon half rose

aren't the same, at all.

'submit' motions to space — and he's
pleasure is his body him lying on
(in) his limbs daily — within
                    him
                    also
                              'inner'
                              on
                    there.
simply — (not if one can't)
                    some
                    times
'places' together outside
wild

                    on the 'present' wild friends
                    are 'there' only, yet not
                              going away
                              either
                    in the middle is their coming
                              together
                    as red leaves sea early rim in
                              oneself
                    or just 'placed' together (to not
                              do that)
                    then its the disparate as rose
                              outside
                              one

wall standing rose could just
                  'place'
                  together
as evening in the middle of
                  people
                  speaking
and so no space even there
                  one?
freezing pale night at wild (only)
                  day
'there' only, no rose even so can
                  'place'
the day there being no people
                  speaking
                  one

It's go in silver freezing
                  half
                  place
the day there being no people
                  and
seeming as them to be, one silver
                  one
                  (not)
any continuum though is at O
                  also
of sun on space at the sky below
separated from its rose sun

Always stay in
the quiet illumined grass
land — but I can't — do it
there being other people there
                    to
                    just do
it only staying in the grass land
                    illumined
'place' it together is 'land' and
                    comes out
                    just
                    do it

He just stays in
        illumined grass land
                    has
        just stayed always in it
                    in
        events going on there and
                    the
                    outside
        of illumined grass land comes
                    out

Always stay in illumined grass
                           land
I didn't see that as a
                              possibility
it's land — just do it — stay

automatons closed barrier where
close to the street in rim in automatons
                           stepping
over people lying night noise hear
                           like
visible barrier blood one dying there
                           only
sneer lead by ill rational barrier half
                              appears
as they're praising each other
no one can   is there

Woman bum murdered, the people interviewed
reassure people will not care there — will not respond

they'll 'get over' woman bum killed
outside
there — not care that being the
effort
to *'not'* respond' — anywhere — is
here? at all (only)

get out of this place

the context
having that done
is
the inner
one
one's dumb
not
separate from
it

that one

freezing evening even
                    is
                    not

(to be)
try that again —
freezing evening even
                    is
                    not

                    I learned the way I learn
something continually is the corrosive mocking from
some one that always bothers me — mocking one
taking
'to be in' 'to approach' or 'seeing' *as* the outside —
that one's is being it — it *is*
                              then
                              (again)
                              or later

                    dusk
        as the outside
one's blood sack   poison
out runs   seen
                    then
        seeing
                    slowed
        isn't seen 'as' one's
                    existing
        and in (their) 'conceptual'
— automatons —   dead

    people move in their middle
                        seen
    sloth is terror in that can't change
    or see   the
                    hell
    land only white land the
                    same
    space fall rose moon place
                    their outside
    always   (anyone)
    changing continually *then* is
                    sloth-
                    terror
                    (only)

                                    one
                                    in (hell)
        changed so as to move into
                                    the
        same space filled with theirs
                                    —

        suffering-movement not seeing
                                    (one's) as
                                    sloth
        terror and unseeing in rose
                                    moon
                                    land
        change to be out   there

                            change the barrier
                                    half
                                    closed
                    side of evening horizontal
                                    hell
                    people in it? without them
                                    can't be
        that. closed horizontal illumined
                                    land-
                                    run

who destroy
                    horizontal
half evening in the same
                    place
people's 'inner'
                    walking
freezing evening first seeing
                    hawk is
hit by car then living
                    (then it
                    is
living) too after and at first
                    seeing,
                    both

appears to be dying
is living too but can't in
                    one's
                    its
                    seeing

the dawn-time but one

which had been hit on
                    the
road flying the freezing
                    evening
                    before

```
the turtle is slow
          I've got it
(by singing)
the turtle is slow
          beat beat                    the turtle approaching
                                           the rose wall?
                                           — OW

                        add
                                                       cello crosses
                            itself in
                                                       space one
                                           the  later one
                     in
                                           society people
                                               when
                            walking                    in
                                               city
                    sloth-terror is on the other side
                                                   from
                                                   it
                            only — can't leave the side




Where is this       Arcadian land she                    says has
been then when we         were there
        taking scathing        cruel    obstructing barrier is
and    "no one felt silenced"— feelings silence? — the
ferocity wasn't                  visible apparent
        (to them)
if Arcadia    occurred where is it      now?    when? if it isn't
now what use is it? changing the past       to praise context
then is phenomena —
                                                   comes out
        is seen occurring in the place       some
```

                                        a
barrier of horizontal evening
closed vertically so there's no past
only it has no side
                                  both
                        evening
                        elation

It's go in
                        horizontal
half evening in the same
                        place
barrier and walking

mechanism of raise
                                  so
                                  no
continuum in them
                                  then
                                  'at'
the same instant any
where then

                                  is
continuum even
                        whereas
they were
                        put outside
                        only
                        'rose'

                                    looking for the falcon diving
                                                            fields
                                                            rose
                                                            at
                        120 miles per hour — we're
                                                            in
                        freezing evening before rose
                                                            too
                                                            there

            The 'present time' is only *my* previous events
    continually — seen (dumb) — then place the present being
    in one (and occurring as one) — conceptual 'also', both —
                wall is 'rose'

                events' space to — 'place' in the same 'space'
                only
                not even the present

                                                    he's
                                not transforming it to
                                                    be lies
                                or being it — stays in illumined
                                                    grass
                                land while seeing
                                                    and in
                                                    fact
                                not transforming
                                                    what occurs
                                                    not separate?

                                                    87

                              to
                                        compare
              'the moon coming into
                                   evening'
              is compared to it/the moon
                                        and to words

                         yet the hawk hit
                                             out it
                   (in fact) got away
                                        'only'

                                        separate
              standing wall of freezing evening
                                        ones
                                        are
              if the mind's repetition at stages one's
              only O rungs sun rose outside of
                                        one's
              junk place waking evening land
                                        have
                                        that
              just — do it — land stay in
                                        comes out

            examin
            ing
dreamed looking down
            in
bush that's huge forest leaveless
            fan
my needing place to live in dream,
            the
            next day
see forest leaveless fans hill up
            vertically
light leaveless array fan
is this the same as

     — is leaves, both — seeing —

            examin
            ing
the forest rose wall as
            white in outside
            and
dark green early forest not different
            from rose
after (it) rose leaveless fan-
            dawn
            one?

                                    hell
                                  -pressure
                                  skin
                    or passages in time
                                  in
          excruciating pain physically so the
                                  time
                                  passages
          are gone. lifted, it's go
                                  so there's
                                  now
          no time here it is spring bare
                                  limbs
          blossom blossoms 'on' bare limbs
                                    'have'
          the blossoms?

                                    seen
          leaveless forest in dream by
          looking   downwards
          so (?) looking up the next day see
                                  leaveless
          fan-forest above
                                  there
          are no 'passages' outside
                                  either
          in time going or one
                                  outside rose
          'after one'

Can't be
in   'night'

as outside it is just 'day one's in'

either time or duration

excruciating physical pain hell
                              night *not*

is there.
'night night'

for Petah Coyne, sculptures/walls, a bird
seen in both sides of one wall
                    and
for Philip Whalen at one time

one is in space and
one is in time

—hell fragment

                    Early
seeing they're walking out as single motions only
at the time nothing numb at the present or
                    that's past.
at barrier of social excruciating is physical that was
                    then. a burst in it in
an   expansive present then.

                                        take
                            numb in intense planned time bursts
                                        — blank
                            automatons for one appears streets
                            people outside walk and like half
                                        visible the ill
                            rational 'given' that's the horizontal
                                        in
                            the same place — as one's excruciating
                                        physical
                            pain is the horizontal also 'night'
                            blackness reef people on the streets to
                            be   tiers
                                        half
                            closed ill dying also there seen directly
                                        by
                            every   'one' can't be
                            changed

Or evening seen in
the same
place
and
people working stifled left by/beside the
ill
rational liked so they're in closed
half
visible barrier only there subjunctive
social
strolling wind. blossoms both 'at' black
there?

even   excruciating physical
side   gut tears there on the half closed
one
blackness reef night
to
adore rational one truncated not one
in visible
'others' tiers of hierarchy that's at once/
both 'experienced'
horizontal spaceless not any in the same
place
there with blossoms,   they're
both —
at both 'night' sides

'bowed line' 'boughed line' pouring
stacks

                  horizon stacks

                  re-
                  place
people's single movement with /and
                  one's
other   spring
outside substituted   is their
        words subjunctive night
                there
                'not inner'
both.

Mechanization. The theory of
the flower is wholly different from
its motion. from a flower moves
within?

        people working stifled stroll carry dirt
        begin to wind on a hill or on evening

        Physical repression so it's on the
                outside of one
        now as walking out is seaming a
                state
        is at once only in one dawn

bullhorns order people in the towns
seeing and pale day-moon on brown
                    peak outside, 'inner'

isn't the opposite   move
everyone *is* excruciating physical pain
on   (only) pale day also

lovely-limitless

She learns others' theories, junk, the
flowers' theories — they
had to do the motions before their
                            existed
is the horizontal 'also night' sole

without they're existing before in half

not in child pale blackish blossom
                        people hated
its motions, those being intellect only at
                        present?
but not that later.

not occurring ever   or there   theory
                              by 'itself'
                              or
only occurring later half early blackish
blossoms *then*
                              half, neither at once
                              the   military
                                     incursions

there one's events are outside only
                                   is
event any 'when' ahead forward *or* is
open appeared state physical child-
                              hood one
can't go to it — any event (to be) has to
                              is with every
event   at once
                              theirs
                              future also

so to entirely 'fill' physical horizon
                              'horizon' *then*
yet can't go to childhood state
                              or
to now   any
                              duration even
present and vertical   hell one
                              half
closed throughout outside *then* moon

man wade in grass
                              by road
to drive is
                                    on one side
                                              axis
axis abandoned the floating day
                                    removed
          it's go in horizontal
          wading in grass
                                        moon
          when moon's not there yet

axis abandoned the floating day

appear with no horizon not black yet

          they're from lightning without
                                              it
          float in the city from day, no
                                                moon
          surfaces there during the day
                                              or
          is
          but without day, lightning, or a

          pool on two evenings, evening is

          embedded in day that's from the
                                        lightning
          abandoned the floating day
                                              then

'his' early-walking
                                    as
'his' 'base-dropping' there is:
                        there is
                        'someone else'
                'theirs' there
one's
comprehending 'there to be occurrence
                        on one side' and
there's no 'side' as moon's in space 'his'-
                        quiet

                                by one's figure
                                evening

in lightning where there is no horizon, only
                                setting
moon and sun at once
axis abandoned the floating moon and sun —

        pool of horses   running
        on immense gold plain but it is indigo sky
                                        that's
        evening horses running in front of far
                                        reflecting
        water lying on the plain, pool where
                                they're
                                running
                                then
        on the floor in evening and lightning

Day Ocean State of Stars' Night

woman says her intent
[as: given— of her]
        is pleasure
while 'we're' bombing
        Afghanistan *then*
—and says that [any] suffering
        depersonalizes that
        one then
        [whoever/them]

woman
                /friend says I don't
                        have
disagreement   when one's
saying one's being
                        attacked by
man/friend [who attack others]. the
        woman says there is no self
in, that is, pleasure—or no self in,
                        her. there.

        their
        suffering   [meaning
        a self]   [as
        not
                        apprehend]
        yet [she says] depersonalized is
                        one is
                        outside
                        [social to her]
        acceptance—   outside
                        being

flying singing
swallows birds
above in
a lit evening
[which is] invisible from singing
beside alongside that child
[spoken of, not there]—an evening or in its next
early day [not there]
are not
higher in
space
than their
[birds] start early evening
then
evenings' early day
one
from them
[many] evenings'
s' one early day.

                    a day
                        is before
                            trays
        [of ocean] heard
                            come on
        the entire thudding
                            rim
                            dawn
                        at dark's
                            cricket
                            sings
                waves from ocean
                            are
                        from the day
        before cricket sings
                            stops in
                    faint lit grass after
                its trays waves [of ocean]
                before [not there place]

        light sheen white cattle before ocean
                            in front of
                                ocean
        thudding of rim—the cattle stand
                    after [not singing]
                    those cricket's dawn
                    in not singing after
                            dawn
                            now is
                        in front of
                    oceans white cattle
                        before it
                    thudding of rim
                        everywhere

                              birds suppressed
                              sing everywhere
                                        in
              light early field before
                          ocean everywhere
                          after [is day]
              wave rolls are on immense
                          [its] ocean sheet where
                                        no
                                    birds
                          sing on green—before—

                              lying as
              weak week—seven—
                          days—
                          nights—
                          aren't—
                          causal—
                          also—
                          black—aside

                                        its
                                    mother
                                    licks
                          white calf
                                    engine
                                    wind
                          doesn't brush
                          them ocean
              before beside behind them there

  coercion

there aren't comparisons in day   already
ahead
anywhere   a hawk is
                                                                                a cycle
the engines—the cycle here passes back and forth between them—

                                                                            not vertical

or horizontal separate at one time—there—hawk cycle streaming

afloat floated between engines beside alongside us driving—in day
                                                                       night road
                                                                  while it being a day
                                                                       2 one's

                                                                       trays of
                                                                  green ocean day
                                                                  green huge ocean
                                                                       state of
                                                                  stars' night

                                                                       day-
                                                                  green huge ocean
                                                                       seen state of
                                                                  stars' night at
                                                                  that night's one early day

Image/Word in *Crowd and not evening or light* and *The Tango*

wading in the grass - it is like an elephant
trunk extended
on the trunk

excreting
crowd and
not evening or light

dreams of people's abandonment
of each other
where
it is beamed into them

as the same

mine goes in and
makes this separation
of them involuntarily
as joy

the nudity of poverty
and calm

scratch
on it

(they) like reality
as a function

scratch on it
scratch on it
scratch on it

not the day being within the blossom

as in reverse (rather than the *day* in it) — the blossom isn't in the *day* either

'not a black dawn/a black dawn' is real-time only.

~

wants to see — 'authority' — of 'other' men — from one, that one would be of only 'them'
there being only 'them' 'so' he is subjunctive

'not a black dawn/a black dawn' is real-time only.

~

beggars whirling in dust fighting
whirling beggars fighting in the dust — while the high rugged brown mountain crags are still, a day-moon is lying on a high brown jutting mountain top. the day-moon and mountain's separation (while the moon is lying on mountain's top) in the high fawn-brown blue atmosphere

is [that] [people's joy]?
a day-moon at the same time as a brown high mountain — their separation

the day-moon lying on the mountain — their separation — it's on high altitude jagged crag desert.

~

military wolves — still shoot the people in a stone-fenced corral open on a brown mountain and bury the corpses in a shallow grave until the families come to pay the army to retrieve them for burial.

military wolves

~

The subject and process in both works (*Crowd and not evening or light* and *The Tango*) can be characterized as trauma in the sense that ordinary event can be experienced as trauma (such as the individual confronting the occurrence of death, the fact of impermanence). But death is ordinary in the sense of applying to everyone. Both poems are a process of viewing layers and divisions, including cognition, sensation, social hierarchy, class, and war. However, if one were to view those phenomena in the category of "trauma," the very division into category determines their experience, as separate from 'normal.' In both of my works here discussed, process is the same as subject: simultaneity and the synonymous nature of mind phenomena and experience (and experiencing). The texts (are to) bring about experiencing (joy) *now*.

Note on *Crowd and not evening or light* (O Books, 1992)

There are seven poem series (including "roll") which precede the final series with photos, titled "Crowd and not evening or light." One segment from the first series titled "roll":

> the dog coming trotting down to the bank — off from
> which — we were in the boat — people bathing off the
> steps — where a — greenish corpse has floated
> —there for burial — to the bank — the dog beginning to eat flesh from
> the buttocks of the body — but not as — our — from the outside
> —the flesh being very soft coming off easily

The segments of the seven series (which are without photos) that precede the title series are (as in the above example) phrases as continuous-fragments creating the sense that a text-segment is spatially flat but also a concave dome (like a snow globe) or a miniature diorama in which the scene, as phrases separated by dashes, conveys space of at once an inside (inner) and outside (as if a text-segment has an outer edge, creating a 3-D effect). The phrases separated by dashes are also 'flat' in the sense of a ticker-tape of single scene of actions ("greenish corpse has floated"—and is eaten by a dog amidst bathing people on the Ganges, for example). The viewer (reader) 'appears' (seems to themselves in reading) to be in the scene, as if the single viewer reading were up close as say in a boat, otherwise they could not have this perspective of the scene: so, the scene duplicates so-called 'natural' optical seeing—yet actually has this dome-effect at the same time—as the *sole* perspective (both at once).

The *image* of the action occurs as its syntax, a folding of 'interior' and 'outside' in space:

the buttocks — of — the corpse — so facing
us, the boats — though submerged, with the soft
flesh of the butt — to the dog — who ate easily — the
bathers in the water — off the steps — close
who're inside — not noticing — I would think

The sense in reading, of there being an interior, is sensation. At the same time, the reader is simply *told* (cued) sensory experience, such as spatial relations in the 'real' scene as if occurring 'in front of' them—for example, cued that the actions are inverted. So, that spatial terrain is mental ('interior') by appearing to be optically seen. Interior as mental is imitated in (by) a scene itself, by elements of the same scene, for example, being repeated in different segments of the poem yet as if "inverted" (changing the perspective of it, not its content or order). That is, the phrases separated by dashes, create the illusion that is a sensation of interior and exterior. The illusion of the ticker-tape single scene as flat with concave edges is similar to the camera's flat sight, or is similar to the sight of the eye, artificial and constructed (as sights seen upsidedown translated by the brain). Thus the phrases of a series' segments imitate consecutive seeing (which itself is a flattening, an abstraction, of occurrences), the implication being that 'linear narrative' is *also* abstraction, construction.

In the series "roll," line breaks and dashes denote how these phrases are to be read (the notation translates the spatial relations as their sound structure). The 'sound' (or space) is apart from content, yet the content exists in no other way. Several of the series of *Crowd and not evening or light* are poem-plays, which are simply designation of the actors' motions in space as also thoughts (in "leg," for example): they say their actions-in-the-present before, after, or while doing them.

Thus that which is 'mental' seems to be an action on its own in a real terrain (real spaces and events), as if 'mental' is an 'element' separate from the actions that are seen (yet only *existed*—as if past—'as' and in these). It seems 'past' though it's only seen *now* in the way it 'appears' in reading.

The miniature (single written segment) appears to contain a vast mass by the effect of this condensation. Condensation entails an entire scene being 'in front of one' yet unfolding and also fixed, in the sense that the same scene is repeated in the writing—by the series' different perspectives seeming fixed as if without changing *inside* (or really)—for a while.

the grueling, deprivation — of
everyone — with it, not a matter of it — so
that it's up to — as many people — as there are
as that as the continual run for the entire — din
—but feeling — so that it is the matter of it

By the 'time' the reader 'reaches' the ending series, titled "Crowd and not evening or light," the viewer is to 'view' (only as text) awareness as occurring in the scene taking place 'in front of' them yet without either the scene or their awareness being visible. *Sensation is only seen outside.* But at the same time the reader approaches this by *having* sensation.

In the series, "Crowd and not evening or light," with photos: There is no miniature—in that, mass is implied by the same public scene (people bathing in shallow ocean) repeated as if *in* the same large space but with few people seen in each flat photo, their unseen (still) actions spread out in no space. The sameness of these actions, and their being incommensurable with *their* language, is or imitates sensation of joy.

The photos and the words (written below, above, or to the side of each photo) are incommensurable but appear to describe and clarify each other. Not only do the words seem to mirror and therefore describe the contents of the photos, but the photos seem equally to be an elucidation of their own apparent captions, the words that are notations hand-written 'on' the photos. Yet they do *not* describe the contents of the photos, which are silence, languageless. Therefore the text also partakes of silence, not having a referent.

(Poem with photo of bathers standing in shallow ocean, a man walking—hand-written:)

> wading in the grass—trunk of woman on the grass
>   in it

> p.60 *(Crowd and not evening or light)*

The text was originally written, and the photos pasted, on blue postcards printed by the Alternative Press, a project in which poets wrote directly on 500 postcards which were to be sent out, thus existing in that form only once by being sent to a single individual. Printed, the surface of the blue card has become invisible. The space has collapsed into the poem series, as translation of space there.

In "Crowd and not evening or light," the 'original' subject (the scenes in the photos) is multiple yet flat as if a spaceless exterior: ocean (not the Ganges River now), standing bathers, sky and ocean the same consistency, no depth or foreground and no action or room for action. The words are the actions—as supposed description, but the objects 'described' exist only as a mental sensation (for example: said of standing bathers in flat ocean without edges, "wading in the grass — it is like an elephant/trunk extended/on the trunk").

The photos are snap-shots, my emphasis is the text. Sitting on Waikiki Beach, I held the automatic camera, intentionally turning it only once or twice, mostly focusing in the same place on the ocean, a flat space into which the bathers would stand or walk.

(Photo of bathers immersed in shallow ocean, one man walking forward—hand-written:)

> excreting
> crowd and not evening
> or light
>
> p. 103 (C)

(People immersed in calm, flat ocean, the same darkness as the sky, one man standing:)

> dreams of people's abandonment
> of each other
> where
> it   is beamed   into them
>
>   as the same
>   p. 68 (C)

Usually the handwritten phrases 'refer' to (or are) something that's only 'one's mind,' not reflecting the phenomena seen at the beach or in the photos. Thus real-time exterior actions are on their own, freed from one. So, the handwritten phrases by imitating one's interior mind-motions are similar to any mind-motions. One is seeing one's mind-motions on exterior space supposedly (that is, it has the sense one is).

Sometimes a handwritten phrase (with photo) 'crosses over' to be 'on' (on the page but also 'on' meaning referencing) the sight (site) that is also the content of its photo, the *exterior content* then being as if the same as the mind-motion.

(Grass and tree trunks before clouds, sky and ocean, people standing/sitting on grass—handwritten:)

> mine goes in
> and makes this separation
> of them involuntarily
>
>   inactive
>   p. 75 (C)

(People, two of them with board, wading out into ocean—handwritten:)

> this isn't on class—wading on grass
> on each other in it

(Darkened cattle—dark on the negative— with white noses pointing, all seated in dark grass, black hill, above which is white light sky—handwritten:)

> floating on those who have—nothing

p. 76 (C)

The developer of the photos somehow scratched some of the negatives of photos, these were a few showing a little boy playing on the rings (at Venice Beach), flying in the air like a gymnast. I retained these scratched photos and drew a pen-line on either side of the scratch (where it reaches the edges of the photo) to emphasize the scratch. The scratch on each photo becomes itself a motion separate from the event seen, a demarcation (of motion above the scratch and of stillness below, for example), and at the same time a negative, voiding what's seen but everything's being there at once.

In one photo, horizontal scratch is a swatch which appears to sweep (which is on the surface) below the curled, flying boy on the rings—the swath of the scratch, marked at either end of its emergence at the sides of the photo by a pen-line outside the edges of the horizontal photo. The text handwritten below the photo is:

> the nudity of poverty
> having — calm

and they say

Another photo is vertical with the scratch running through the boy's body curled in space centered in the air. There is little difference seen between sky and sand between which he flies. The pen-line, emphasizing the scratch, seems to extend it downward (though the scratch is also seen, 'known,' to be neither downward nor upward, neither 'in' nor 'on' the space):

> the nudity of poverty
> and calm

scratch
on it

It's sense of writing on reality: 'One' is doing so. The handwriting is 'like' anyone's. Another scratched photo—the scratch to one side of the flying boy who's almost centered in space of sky hardly different from sand—shows double scratch extended as pen-marks at the top and bottom edges of the photo. The handwritten words are:

>(they) like reality
>as a function

>>scratch on it
>>scratch on it
>>scratch on it

Note on *The Tango* (published by Granary Books, 2001, 10 in. wide x 13 in. height)

I began the poem sequence, titled *The Tango,* before taking a trip to Tibet and continued the writing after leaving Tibet (unable to cognate in the high altitude, traveling through the country for three weeks). Visiting the Sera Monastery located outside Lhasa, I watched the young monks in formal debate. They are asked traditional questions from the Sutras by a monk who in assuming this role tends to harangue and prod a small group who remain quiet considering. There were various such small groups of young monks gathered here and there in an outside debating court. The questioner will then clap his hands in a dance-like gesture signifying the instant in which they are to respond with individual answers derived intuitively.

Watching, I compared these debates, at once interior and social, the appearance of their debating process, to the gesture of my poem which is internal debate synonymous with shadow of social actions enacted, and as reading, going on in one (both reader and writer), the writing being location-notation: of that which is anyone's divisions of memory, present, occurrence, emotion—all these as *a* space, as phrases separated by dashes and paragraphs.

I shot four or so rolls of film, both color and black and white, pointing the camera on a small group, shifting to another such group, attempting to get the instant of the clapping of hands, turning so that what appears in a photo's frame is at random whether the subject is rose-colored folds of their robes, their faces, hands, or feet. The photos are placed (in the order in which they were snapped—that is, in the monk's activity) in vertical strips in the book, next to the vertically unfolding text sequence, written separately in its mind-activity of an internal debate that was only my own. The writing (separate from the photos) examines and questions one's being as both synony-mous with occurrence/memory/emotion/ seeing—and (as) these, at the same time, being separate from each other.

The line breaks, which are part of the poem's sound structure as phrase, were deter-mined by my starting the text at a far right margin on the page: the line breaks are thus an invention or a procedure of the collaboration itself, determined by mechanically starting each segment at a far right margin on the page to make space for the photos. Thus the two mediums are merely placed in their own orders of occurrence side-by-side without being illustrations. Nor could the visual and the text illustrate each other—in that I could not understand Tibetan: I was only responding to the monks as *seen*. Yet the activity of the poem is a mental debate in 'one' (reader/writer) which trans-lates words for phenomena. The word "rose," for example, appears to 'cross over' as a translation directly of the monks' rose-colored robes, but is also a verb as well as a ref-erence to the flower.

> pink roses — aren't the pink sun rising — are 'social'
> *only?* Both
>
>   . . .
>
>   — to make these be the same 'in order' to dis-place
> 'them' and one
>
>   'in order' — in spring, later — both.
> as it not being first, but at the same time.

To make a past event be 'placed' in the present (as if it is a sight viewed) 'in order' (in sequence) to dis-place both (both the present and past): Order of sequence is main-tained yet it is actually the displacing of past and present as the act of seeing (as read-ing) both as being 'once' (at once).

One particular childhood memory (of the writer's: placed alongside the sight of the monks speaking) is cited: seeing a starving man dying (during a famine), who is lying in garbage on a dock near a ship. One is alone walking past him on the dock. A ques-tion of the text is the relation between observation and emotion, being and history: Emotion is causal, is itself event and causes event. Yet "emotion is not the cause of impermanence." Oneself is not separate from (being) observation (seeing and analysis) and emotion (response in reference to the early event of seeing the starving man), but one is not that event, though it *constitutes* one's memory: "one will not be event" (future).

One's task is not simply to *recover* from an event, in that one takes place *as* such, an event which is provoking and altering. The task undertaken is to *be* (in relation to it).

Memory restates the conditions of its occurrence (that's what a memory *is,* merely reproduces), thus may entrap one in a cycle of response. The poem by 'placing' past, future, and present together ("both"—a pair of future and past always, in that present is empty as being only the action of reading, of attention) is a thought process whose import (the process itself) is to abandon time. If time is abandoned, event is not based in time. However, free-floating memory might reproduce itself infinitely. Therefore the poem seeks to separate sight from image and to separate thinking, as these occur, from the ground (or basis) that was their origin—so as *"not* to re-state conditions even. (those conditions are not the/ground even.)." The writing's gesture is to allow memory to exist there in it (not to base thought process in repression or destruction of self) but to free it from its constant reproduction of its conditions, by openly doing the mental construction that repeats its own conditions allowing the two to co-exist separately together (construction and subject). Visual image is memory, the sight of the starving man. It is also actual (new) sights, the sight of and the photos of the monks debating, and all sights seen at present.

I composed a note that's on the (artists' collaboration Granary) book's back cover describing the poem as reading. It's intended as part of the poem. This poem 'proceeds' by occasionally *exact* repetition of a phrase:

"The text's internal debate is the author's comparison of *her* mind phenomena to exterior phenomena, laying these alongside each other actually—such as the mind's comparison to dawn, to magnolias, to color of night, as if these are manifestations of mind phenomena, which they are *here.* Placing one's mind-actions beside magnolias (words). The same figure repeated everywhere, a line or passage may recur exactly as slipping out of, returning to, slipping out of, a frame of concentration and sound."

As *text,* visual image (phenomena such as black dawn and memory) and image as word are given as the same simultaneity, these (dawn, memory, optical seeing) existing separately and also abandoned as such. The implication is that if words as perception are also phenomena (if "rose" is a verb and a color at once, and if it is *only* a word—but is at once also a "flower") there *are* no images other than 'dismantling itself', dismantling of (pre)conceiving seeing and thinking at once. Language could be actually shreds that are mind, rather than already socialized images (socialized images are even those phenomenally seen—which would be *anything* seen, such as flowers): Seeing is *there* impermanence as such.

> is subjunctive — the man starving dying lying in
> garbage? — there not being black dawn — ?
> no. not anyway — that is, anywhere. — or:
> subjunctive is *only* 'social.' both.

then (when alive). — (subjunctive.) — black dawn
isn't? — so it has to pass. both.

The writing 'appears' as a physical phenomenon (such as magnolias, roses, or words) alongside mind phenomena (words, thoughts). The writing apparently demonstrates or is demonstrated by the monks' activities, as seen in the photos (suggested in that the viewer is viewing these sights while reading)—but actually, by itself, the writing as only the viewer's mental activity is 'seen' separately.

This characteristic of 'reading being seeing one's own mental activity' occurs in the text by itself (without the photos) by the effect of words occurring with all of their alternate meanings at once ("rose"—which is verb, flower, color) and in the phrases of the writing separated by dashes and paragraphs that compare each other, as well as repetition that is exactly the same phrase, same 'scene' occurring again in a different space.

not the day being within the blossom

as in reverse (rather than the *day* in it) — the blossom
isn't in the *day* either

'not a black dawn/a black dawn' is real-time only.

———————

wants to see — 'authority' — of 'other' men — from
one, that one would be of only 'them'
there being only 'them' 'so' he is subjunctive

'not a black dawn/a black dawn' is real-time only.

Surrealist Max Ernst described the artist's action of one eye being closed looking inward simultaneous with one eye open seeing the outside as the artist's realistic synthesis of both inner and outside worlds at once. Coincidentally, perhaps my comparisons of 'one's' mind phenomena simultaneous with (as) outside is akin as analysis of one's seeing. A statement of *The Tango's* action (and intention) is given in one phrase: "to change location's relation to construction of meaning." By this I meant: Change the space/the place in space (also society—which is also conceptual grasp as shape of thought only *there*). Change placement of phenomena in space that is only the writing, such as the moon 'in' night or 'in' day—in the writing's space/word. The phrases are 'directly' mind shreds placed next to each other, an abstraction of my mind as action (as reading, thinking, memory, and distinction-making *there/while* distinguishing) that goes on as 'one' reading (attention in that space as the instant of reading—so the 'space' is also the instant of the reader's time). As a comparison of mind phenomena, as also socially constructed in action, to outside, the 'between place' that's the text is a synthesis that might (is to try to) apprehend (and be) outside of mind at once (as it is *being* mind).

> to ignore one's shape/events 'so' it goes on wildly —
> *and* — anyway.

> words 'black dawn' as shape (instance that has no
> 'other' occurrence) which is 'their shape/and their *conceptual*
> shape.'
> to subordinate magnolia buds — that is real-time —
> both.

While citing military and repressive actions as seen in Tibet, *The Tango's* surface includes this experience as simultaneously 'experienced' in one's condition in the US, manifested even as early experience of divisions, the making and the keeping in place of those divisions. One is being translated even as the conception of one changing the outside as (by) changing oneself.

> bound as 'split' (one's) 'to' conception of change as, or
> in, behavior —
>> that was not when a child
>> so 'split' is *that* only — ocean 'in' blossoming trees —
> 'in fact' has to be to change people's behavior/one's as sole

The text is a space that substitutes itself for (as) physical sensation and motions in space. These motions are thus future, occurring there as to be a present-experiencing ('joy'). The images of the photos (folds of robes, body and facial gesture) do this also as a still present. Some of my texts (such as the poem *way*) are abstraction of motions, motions as being within minute events and being at once series of events as history. Their sense of physical gesture is synonymous with conceptual. Motions (abstractions as events—would thus be always *past) are* new relation (to each other) outside. My intention is for text to be, and also at once apprehend, these new relations.

— one's subjectivity/language is their or one's *motion*
only there?

    seeing being only a motion even (in walking, say)
    one has no back — yet. — not even 'in' 'night' —
not even past movements' 'night' — either — and is
    future 'nights'
    where(?) no movement of one's occurs — future is
same as one's motions without extension *now*

    one's motion ahead — is only one *now* —nights rose

In that thinking and image are the same in the text (the same *as* text—visual image such as "rose" and that as word), the intention is apprehension outside of one's images and other social ordering.

    the fabric of their logic (itself hierarchy) is a 'whole,'
which they say is
    'analysis.' — one's 'analysis' of their 'whole' fabric,
they say is a 'whole'
    (in order to dismiss it) or they say is "insane" *but it
can't be both* probably
    convention of perception — can't be both 'whole' and
'insane' — unless it's theirs (they construct)

    they exclude outside

Analysis is not separate from the seeing and thinking that is the process of the text. My use of analysis, which is removing image by using image, could (is to) never be a 'whole' fabric— which if it were would replace or override actual phenomenal action. Similarly, reference in the poem to social violence is to the images constructing one-self—here—now.

(Beside photo of young monks seen speaking:)

    ears are as if lips — *but ears 'are' lips.* trunk as man's
chest. woman's ears lying back as she lies down. forward
trunk floating or lying on ears
    people charging make interior motion 'outside'

The Forest is in the Euphrates River

For the sculptor Petah Coyne, and for poet Judith Goldman

>not a mirror
>the forest is in the Euphrates River

The outside   floor
                                         completely

                                         harmonious

peoples on the rose desert

                cruising Toyotas

                break the delicate surface

so the rose huge floor goes

everywhere the rose floor of streets

                                         with people
                just the outside (word) is harmonious,

                                         though it is

Oarsmen/Eye/Forest—(Reading as Horizontal Sights)

Their looking from their eyes (theirs being plural) 'is' in the middle. One's eye is in the middle. One's/they're in the forest (thus silent words). One is walking. The floor of the forest, black rose-sewage, floats then. Then black roses and fur grow floating, oarsmen row the forest. No sky is there.

Hospice did not allow treatment that would lead to remission, either chemotherapy or radiation. Knowing this, and hearing the mother state she wanted to live wanted to consider treatment, her youngest daughter arranged for hospice, without discussion with family and without the mother's knowledge or consent, to begin before the first meeting with the oncologist. The daughter announced this as a fait accompli to her next older sister who stuttered But we are seeking treatment…There will be no treatment, the younger sister declared.

The floor of the forest is the door (of the black train of roses). This isn't a dream but the rule is (it has a rule though it's not a dream, though it is free floating, undetermined): if black roses and fur grow, the oarsmen are rowing them there. Just seen. So they'd say this is nothing.

There aren't edges or periphery either. One's eye being in the middle sometimes sees the oarsmen but if they are close to blank eye they are invisible. Present they're oaring forest but *there they're* invisible. A word is still always.

The forest isn't black. Its train crusted black roses and fur. A face rose weeping. The face is seen only at random. It may be in blank eye still. Who is in the middle of the forest. Besides one. There aren't going to be any questions because the president has blinded them there.

But still and without there being a word one in the middle of the forest, therefore blank having only future, has that *then*. At the time.

One hasn't dreamed since her family, led by the third daughter suddenly assuming being its head, bullied her and their mother who had a brain tumor. Were also bullying the exhausted and frightened father, though sustaining him alone. It floats as a plate on the surface. When the mother is scanned and seen to have a brain tumor, the third daughter—unknown to the second daughter—has herself named as next in line to replace the father in determining the mother's care if he goes away. This should only take effect if the mother is unconscious, yet the third daughter acts as if the mother is unconscious now. The father keeps going away. The family concurs to oppose treatment of the elderly mother, who'd taken the treatments faithfully. Again. Earlier, unformed who'd turned into a minotaur intercedes insisting to the grieving father the mother is not in her right mind when she indicates intent to treat the illness, the unformed secretly securing a document giving herself authority over her mother's life, as if the mother were unconscious when she is not, should the father not be there. He keeps going away.

The father, without telling the second daughter and her lover about the existence of that document (is a forest of petals—no), asks them to arrange and draw up a document placing himself solely in charge, which would unseat the third daughter from this role without saying he is doing that to her. Because who could come up against her. Yet he relies on her to care for him daily in everything.

One goes against the unformed minotaur for the first time.

The hatchling minotaur can force because she is encouraged by Iago. The forest is the black-rose floor only. The hatchling, spewing, revved into another gear lies to the others—yet in front of one they appear not to even care if this is true—maintaining mother was being forced by one to be treated.

The others care about her mother. Are the elderly not listened to. Our—regarded as not there already. They conceive of her as elderly—It is in spring, it is spring.

One can't dream, yet later one dreams the woman who gored is sitting in a car as if planting herself in front of the house in which they'd grown up. The gorer is boasting to someone else—the same man who, with her, outside the dream, commented on the uniform process of all death, ascribing this to the mother, who lay listening and ceased to speak after this episode, either because the words had discouraged her or because she would have ceased to speak then anyway. The gorer's smug tone in the dream speaking to him in front of the house is usurping by condescension, the same tone she was using *outside* the dream of possessing and of being everything in a family in which devotion is central and one non-existent outside of expending that. So, it is the assumption of the dream also, which an outsider who 'saw' this dream occurring could not comprehend in it, that the family house is all. *As childhood*. (Though the people in the dream are adults.) The gorer having taken over the house of their childhood (from which the parents outside the dream had moved long before) occupies everything. At all. Not that she (one) wanted ever to be in childhood only, as does the gorer—but one's existing as it arises in childhood has to be *entirely* relinquished to someone else. Yet the second woman (one) is now not in either the family or in the outside. Why does she see that she is no longer in the outside.

There have been two contradictory directives outside the dream, which it is indicating: *Only being in the family*. (And thus non-existent otherwise.) And the simultaneous directive: *Only being outside*. (Not only is the outside the objective but the family hardly exists, in the second directive. One's reversed into the outside.)

The gorer has only one of these directives. She does not have the directive of one being *only* the outside. She 'lacked' it, a question as to the word 'lacked,' though there are no questions. For the gorer, in goring and in being blinded—by the president as we are—the outside does not exist.

A fine rose silt fills the air in day and night here. The Sahara is being broken down now by Toyota Cruisers used by everyone the nomads cruise the desert and break its delicate crust which disturbed enters huge sand storms that obscure the ball in space's atmosphere because the rose desert below as its floor is huge. The Toyotas cruising tearing the rose train, it is now everywhere. The rose train of those cruising causes illness in people's now rose lungs and in rivers of their eyes, black at night.

There's no way to directly articulate. A blind fascist having only personal life— that's what a fascist is *here*. The coercive hatchling minotaur shouted. The internal events occur while the second daughter is without words. How has the other one had only personal life here. A bully or fascist 'is' as if they were interchangeable because there aren't words here. They sneered as a pack as if they were expressing feeling and as if one, in favoring treatment, were criminal in which the bully was sustained, speaking so that blank couldn't speak, speaking when one spoke.

One's family now hates her. The minotaur boasts to one that they all hate her, spoken as the minotaur traipses in front of her. Except the father, wanting treatment silently in front of the family in the midst of their actions to one. Yet not silent in that he agreed to treatment with the doctors and says this to *one. It doesn't matter what they think!*—about this—what they think about one—he takes her aside and says.

The ignorant bully knowing nothing of this illness, she thinks eating bananas fed by one is killing her mother, who'd have the mother die at once (yet mother had treatment which shrank the tumor to be a very small size—against the hatchling minotaur's will), and who aloud in front of the mother after which the mother becomes entirely silent says: Her skin is breaking down everywhere—pointing out process of all death where the mother had just said to one *Then we'll try!*—hates one in this, arising then, at the point of the start of the mother's illness. Now.

A man, clear, says people dying have to deal with things that happen when they're dying. Bad or good, it's what's occurred (now past), for that person. There isn't present seemingly: 'Too' is wordless. And is also. Now is folded over in space. There she flips her wild sides silently beside the family.

The shock hurts her. It appears that they don't have any sense of anybody being free.

For Iago, family is only tyranny which she (Iago) uses. Iago says to her (one), as if she were not, It is time to be mature, in the cold black desert.

Our insane maturity is—one is the outside as being, and one is 'the outside is entirely rejected.' Iago conflates these to one is only forced by the outside, one rejecting it therefore (which is oneself) but *being it* as *its convention only.*

this is not bud. bud   is

(lineage)

                    unborn   is there at once

          a horizontal night.

If the mother can't be cured there is either only 'personal' or only 'being outside.'
And family is not 'personal.' Outside the forest. Also. The sun goes down as one is
walking, at dusk.

                    once. recurring. first

                    drones

                    floating

                    are killing the insurgents   who're

                    everyone   there
                              the only thing to be is the insurgents

                    people cruising the rose desert surface is broken

                    by beside Toyota cruisers   also

                                                  is rose black night also

                    black rose-sewage train so one's by   not from

                    roof sewage-forest

Therefore there's an empty spot where the eye which is her eye also at once is in the
forest. Having entered, the red sun isn't visible there. She would walk anyway, at
night also. Yet in the middle, one can't dream either. Seven doctors say the mother's
pain would be alleviated by radiation though she will die only slightly later than if
not treated. One doctor says No one knows when a person will die. Do it. Seeing the
oarsmen is separate, has to be at the same time (that is, in the future only). Has to
dream there, one feels. Dreams are only accessing one's own frame, which is stopped
here, completely unlike.

C

Circe seduces others, charms without her sensation or touch there, other than her words, which flatter men in *their* hierarchies only. So she creates these in people who would not ordinarily do it. As if other women did not exist, the forest is in the Euphrates River. These two are not panels of each other. Some women are flattered by her but only to facilitate. Everyone facilitates her then. C gives them nothing else. Than their flattery. They don't see this. Feeling disgust for sensation, also wanting to have power (which seems the other part of not having sensation), in C, are invisible to these men, who also want power but as black roses fur furl in a flood in the thin forest, and there feel sensation. Fuel. In C's flattery, people seeing her only in their hierarchy turn: A man turns into a deer, or a white pooch, another man into a small owl. Thin on a green forest, they have simple features. Not flying or running. They're snubbed.

Seated on the dark, now hot forest rosefur-floor, the pooch appears to have a simple, flat body much smaller than C. How one wonders does C copulate with them. C is elderly almost. But these are lovers. Would C one wonders copulate with them before they've changed to be separate from her (in their being an owl or deer). Or before the separation in her being almost elderly. Yet before a small owl in the tree copulates with C's white, fooling with her flat, floating belly lying in the green shimmering forest pulls the long, heavy stem up in C and comes, it rose. From her belly, while C does nothing with or to the owl. C came on the heavy stem the small owl had been on her. There is a small space between that is ecstatic. One thinks the *action* only. In the future C comes, from the owl, maybe before it changed to be that, as a quiet man, but this is just in the future *here*. The small owl comes on her belly just in *their* future, known only to them. Under the wire.

At that same time, one is beside the deer-body of a man, lying beside her at night (lying beside *him* each night)—only his body projected as a deer as weight—mounting the brush leaping flames in their fleeing the forest-fire.

As a bulbous, blood-red sun lowering below the earth. There is a space that is not available to them, like the green meadow between, for example, but is between in spaces there.

One isn't being sarcastic. (Referring to C copulating.) Because it's a thin plate. Flesh and translucent something. A stretched cowhide with pierced, lashed wounds, which weeps occasionally, is there.

C asks to hire one to find someone, and asks her to do secretarial work. But one isn't a detective or secretary. C is imitating one. At a present moment she changes one's thoughts in what blank says to be something else—C imitating blank but altering it in front of others. Thus, for C, history is passive, without actions even. Always already altered. Yet C cannot change blank's body to be something else (such as a deer) in that one isn't a man. For C, men are separate, superior, though blank can't comprehend this as it makes no sense, isn't there. The moon squeezes. The ripple of the black night is before it, yet the round moon is before there was a black ripple. There's the sound of a crowd rushing, or swept into walls. Nearby. That is the black ripple on which or beside which vertically hangs and floats moon as a white iris sticking to the surface lens of one's eye. The pigment of blank's enflamed irises comes off in bright flecks on the walls of the eyes.

Concerned about the second's turmoil, seeing it and that it stemmed from herself dying, the ill mother had called out cautioning the second daughter who's leaving the house once, Enjoy being in your life. This is the instruction for this as well as to dream. Helplessly (may be—anyway, on one's own, with friends if one can *see* them—they're there).

It's called a black 'sea' of roses. For a black 'ocean' is weight. Ocean is rain. Ocean in rain *is* rain. C in the rain (the ocean that's coming down) is soundless too, her charm nullified in that that night no one is around, she's smoking a cigarette. Graceful dipping her legs stretched down from a chair in night. Rain 'at' night is that black ocean around blank with nothing but waves. The Euphrates River is the forest's choppy black waves that are not in water.

Excruciating physical pain (when it had occurred) that is one's enflamed frame within one's skin, the spine a cord in the back—so it's neither inside nor outside anywhere—is at the same time (as the outside, in its being oneself) and is at once spring in that the trees blossoming everywhere are *then,* is there. One's formerly broken spine is outside then. Then the enflamed irises that are eyes are outside also. The blossoming trees outside them/the trees—seen have no pain. In the sense that they (the blossoming boughs, trees in them—a tree is in its blossoms then) have no feeling then, are not enflamed yet are the extreme in space present where nothing dies there. Oneself when it's excruciating pain is out alongside they're blossoming. It is not feeling there. Is to one. Is spring just then. Not outside that.

This happens now in one's enflamed eyes. The small, curled mother in the bed is alongside oneself in space. Speaking to her is there (is the inside) the only place in space in spring.

C is a civil servant. Doling out posts, she appears to have caused the future or control it in having many supplicants with no present existing. Thus no future is here either (it's described insolently), the president also at once (differently) turning the crowd into 'our' stupid, blind, gutted ones. There's no anarchy going on. But this is not visible here. Our soldiers in Fallujah where we live—no, we don't live—there now bomb and mow down the people demolishing the walls of the city. The streets are filled with the dead who are thrown into the Euphrates River because there are too many. Their stench and decomposition swam in the streets, in the rose-sewage. Everyone is an insurgent if they live. There. Yet they are to be invisible dead here.

The rose desert   is being

                                                                         torn up

by

floor

the cruisers   the people cruise them on

                                          the rose sand desert's surface

in Toyotas

                                                            break its surface

which enters the ball in space's

                                                                              there

                                                              with the desert

The Forest is in the Euphrates River

C does not think about this. Because I say/don't imagine so. She is flat, one-dimensional creamy lying in the forest with the owl: But she is *telling lies* also. Small posts are doled out by Circe to men who, being the only visible men, are easily turned by her. There's competition. Periphery not existing in space, visible men corrupted by sinecures (there is such a thing as 'corruption'—and perhaps C can't imagine this way of thinking) speak on their own periphery of hearing. C does not have much power, the posts being insignificant, if you ask me, yet the effect because of her being *without* force (outside of it, from the outside) is the change of another into a small, white, muted with simple features, pooch. Who may be at the same time a violent man. Or deer with dull, soft eyes on crafts of boat-bodies by which (their bodies) the deer are still, are seen from the oarsmen in the middle oaring the black-rose-sewage-floor-forest with no sky. Not by, *beside* the oarsmen. One's eye. They row by C perhaps (there are no questions asked—as our president blinded us). That is, *when* he did.

no sky. Not by, *beside* the oarsmen. They row by C perhaps (there are no questions

That lead-bully female appears, is translated, as a minotaur when in bullying (imagination), is utterly different from C by minotaur using savage force devoid of charm and by her being a different person. Who are the Brownshirts. Asks a man, dubious and suspicious, That this is real. Thinks it is. Mother is to be swept wordlessly away, she's swept wordlessly.

She stopped speaking. Yet utterly embraced, adored.

The minotaur female to possess father swivels on her bulging shoulders, there is to be no anarchism, anarchy. Her wild sides in bulk traipsing stalks pouring mouth shouting at one. Woman Iago holds an apple of discord to throw it in, shooting blank looks of hatred, one will not be speaking aloud, again. 'Not again' at all is anarchy. If this occurs in death. Of anyone, of anyone else. (Or anarchy if speaking does not occur again in their lives.) While father is silent, except in the background to one, favoring treatment for mother, and seemingly paired with third daughter, one is to take the hit. The minotaur traipsing bulges her face and shoulders pouring out from her mouth not from her head.

Repeating is a cold desert.

The humped hunched trotting and swiveling the huge shoulders and head which on the trunk with its rolls of fat tapers to spindling traipsing legs, each on a hoof—is extended in air shouting that's just in the mouth. Not in *one's* head either (in hearing), vitriolic spews in the air from the humped trotting. Whose only humped rage trots there. Back and forth in front of one.

The traipsing coiled rolls shouting had groomed her offspring to do this also—a daughter appears in the air, shouting over the phone that one advocating treatment to alleviate had *caused* mother's suffering, before the treatment begins.

But mother took treatment then.

Pulling back unrelated to anything, C is utterly successful, which is only irrelevant to one now. It *should* be irrelevant. A pooch waddles to C, only because transformed it has short legs.

This means there isn't anything as expression (here). Thus exposed as conflict how can this be anything (it can't be seen). For conflict is nothing, if only itself. We're taught. It is. The floor-forest is there fan of the oarsmen then. When. If it's only conflict, it's what we were doing always though. Apparently. There are just posts (positions) mirroring boards stuck in the desert floor. One hasn't a post, though she can't focus on it in this case. And are seen *from* the oarsmen (it's coming from them and from their or one being there). What are And. They're not blank but active space. And. And is rain, the ocean-floor with no floor. It's white rain, the snowing floor.

Whose conflict occurs in exactly the same way the outside is occurring. The violence of the minotaur with her swinging bulk body the sides traipsing shouting lies (she's lying in air) is to reverse her (minotaur's) own actions and behavior into being one in blank violence: That one is supposedly doing, has done, what the other in bullying is doing is interpreted to the others (their same family), never *'to'* though in front of one as if one had never existed. Therefore blank seeing this is not one doesn't matter. It's in Baghdad amid the US soldiers. Separately. In front of one, lying in air. One doesn't live then. Outside of this does doesn't.

Now nothing seems to move but the rose-black forest moves fast while everything is blank (at the sides).

Death doesn't exist. Mother'd said intensely Why can't *I* survive. *You've* had things happen to you and *you've* survived. My children have survived, why can't *I*. Or she said: My children have survived, yet *I* can't. She paused, then she said We just *have* to survive—that's all there is. There is no mortality. She didn't. Couldn't. Yet one has to alter this, but can't dream still yet.

They all meet in a room and silence one, speaking before I can speak. I'm not allowed to speak. After, the shaking, silent father takes me aside and when I cry They blame me for mother's suffering! who's alive lying in the next room, he exclaims *It doesn't matter what they think!*

The Circle on the Intestine

Their hatred coming from the lies uttered by the gorer, it is jealousy occurring at death. Around its time.

Her technique is to bottle up another and then attack. The woman who smirks. When mother was ill a circular incision formed from punctures of the minotaur's horns on one's belly.

Red liquid expands on the edges of the circle squirting the outside of one's abdomen and intestine. While horning, rolled minotaur smirking that everyone hates one derided blank if the latter rose from her chair during it.

Minotaur says to their father who was seated watching quietly there: You can see I'm being polite whereas she (one) is angry, when one rose from one's chair.

Claims jeering to blank that she kids herself— "You *think* everyone's against you"— as if it were her own deluding ego: Whereas, the gorer condescends, no one's spoken of you with each other (supposedly)—while, nevertheless, everyone agrees they hate you, according to the mouth, which utters anything. Cruelty is polite, it thinks, it twists its floating hoof.

To lunge lying in air. Frightened the mother would live (it is one's theory now), the minotaur female had had to possess the ill one there in order to possess the father. Outside the boat-bodies float on the street of deer turned from men. Getting up in the dark at morning—though it's the green city during day—it's the day cold black desert.

The tsunami occurred at this time. A wave through one ocean after another. The wave withdrew the floor-ocean far back from a beach, then ascended over it curling fifty feet above in the air, drowning hundreds of thousands from countries, carried out to sea hanging on wreckage. Later, many hanging in mid-ocean were picked up by ships. Red Cross workers wrapped masses in blue plastic body bags. Later one thinks to the minotaur You think you possess the floating being (not dead, changeable)—who by that time has disappeared though he's there for the minotaur only—his the not dead changeable has something to do with forgiving, (him) later one thinks.

The mother watched the tsunami in the news. There's the desert in mourning after her death which seemed sudden. This is in the city at day, also at the same time the cold dark desert even in light at day it's clear dark with nothing there, people move around though, the boat-bodies of deer moving through the dark crystal light.

The gorer who had at first when the mother was diagnosed overwhelmed her sibling (one) with a lava of hatred, trying to push that other from the room to try to eliminate her, hovered presiding on their mother to possess her by sucking her from life, apparently. None of the arrangements are known to one. It's as if sealed. In one being excluded from this, sealed into it.

She maintained immediately the mother asking for treatment is not in her right mind (repeating is the cold desert now, despair). In order to prevent treatment, the third daughter says to the father What's the difference between a month and a year more of life. Eleven months, one thinks. The gorer moves in, nesting on the premises, strangely dictating *I'm—the—*daughter, she says into the phone. Iago's another daughter but tests by holding the apple of discord to throw it in from a distance in order to see what will happen, occasionally feeding the gorer (minotaur is more stupid than Iago) engineering on a flat plate her wild sides. They play with each other. They organize their offspring.

Blank had never had this thought of them before. Now, while it's going on, it won't go away.

It's like spawning though the offspring are born, are there. But on a mirror in dark crystal light.

Hops is the traipsing large bulk on a crystal dark clear plate in front of their father she's speaking any cruel words to one that have arisen in the mouth. She already gores but no scene like this has happened before, between the goring and blank.

Before the mother was ill, this action hadn't been translated. Goring does not remember what she's said, or says in the same sentence apparently, in that there're no words.

Though Iago had exuded poison to both, to everyone. Her own offspring became Iago's ministrants. To be not in the stream of ministrants, ministering.

An Action

Gray rain was a straight falling ocean everywhere, the air horizontal inside it. The air that was is the falling ocean paused for a day or two. They went to the cemetery in the pause ocean between the horizontal air raining and itself vertically falling.

The burial occurred in a cold dewy green country cemetery. The others, not speaking to her as they were directed by their mothers, who were there (directed in everything—it would be a question but the president blinded us—everything *there,* what's seen), crowded to throw dirt on the coffin lowered into the ground. The father frail and trembling, helped by grandchildren, walked to the grave, a silent wail coming only visibly from him when they threw the dirt. They drove away. Driving on the ocean road, out-before-constricted other leaving mother there with dirt covering her! and T see that the others have turned on a mountain road, so they turn around to drive back and follow them. Is speaking about the burial to him. There is no one speaking inchoate yet is wild. At all, because of that. At a curve, which is a pull-off, on the winding road is a huge coyote standing.

They pull over, stop and look at it. The coyote eyes as if toward her using force crosses its front paws in front of itself and bows by dragging its thick neck down one leg with its neck twisted to look slanted eyes at her intensely while dragging the neck up against the other leg from the ground again—in a deep bow. The words occur to her *as* the coyote bows—presented [she thinks of] words "It *is* all right," words which are from, in the sense of in front of, or are beside the wild animal uttered by it yet as a weak translation occurring sarcastically transpiring to her.

The coyote comforted me. Then turning, yet it twists its head to look at her impression at first of sarcastically over its shoulder again, it disappears off the ledge of the road into the forest.

Questioned, T says It bowed. Furthermore, you didn't know you were going that way (on the mountain road) and it was there when you came that way, for that. A friend who's a doctor, surprised, says It was your mother! Maybe she said meant It came from your mother! We're a second only. Second thinks It came from the coyote. That would be seen as a question except the president has blinded us. Or it comes at death from occurrence itself, like their jealousy.

Their jealousy is of her existence even, unrelated to her though overtime related to her nature, thus to her actions outside (apart, overtime, from any actions in relation to them).

How does it (the gesture) come from the coyote. If nothing moves. She's so stunned by her mother's death. Or from the dead. T says I stopped because I knew it had something to say to you, the way it looked. Because anyway it (the coyote's action) came from some other event, if only from the event of her perception from death. Whose perception. Is connected in space. Is its bowing not an accompanying event to hers. Or is its first, with the death.

Now she notes the fact that the coyote's action, evident and directed to her—from its facial expression—is in relation to it being outside the range of her personality (also! no), that she would not believe such a thing and therefore could not think to produce it.

Nor does she produce goring but she sees it though she's blinded in the enflamed irises. Days, going to take the mother to her radiation appointments she crazily slowly drives the car ahead of her irises, that are afire. Or rather, she is *behind* her irises. The enflamed irises are first.

Goring

Goring had transcribed in space: someone else is doing the thing (that actually *she* in goring was doing). The others hold in reference the transcribed version. But it is because they choose to.

The gorer had looked only at their father while she'd savaged the other, her mouth uttering whatever cruel word comes into it rather than the stream of words even first entering in her head.

And, as if to divert and thus convince him with lies even were success, her apparently having the sense that the occurrence (and the reaction of the one savaged) doesn't exist at all apart from his view, is only a reaction reflected in him which can be obliterated if he *shows* no reflection of it, he did not show any, seated. But he is elderly shaken. Then.

Like spring the event is not seen. Ever. Except by blank. By a second. Certainly the gorer is neither a boat-body nor a seducer like C, rather is gross force without intervention affecting her except fear. Iago had removed the hatchling minotaur's fear. That was new. Always has to have someone with the minotaur, someone accompanies her, to overwhelm any there.

Since one no longer has a family a thought arises first.

The other, blank in the sense that is spring, is exposed to an unavoidable, unbeatable thought. Both frightening and exciting. One friend phrases it, in regard to this situation: to be without the imagination. That thought is: the necessity to not have, by undoing all before in events outside in oneself, any authority retroactively *in* the outside before and in the present.

This thought had arisen before, but it occurs differently now. What's important is to bring about seeing that difference by seeing its relation to this instant only. The nation is horizontal. The sky is. There are only present actions in that sense. So, anyone's actions are not behind anything. The minotaur uttering any cruel words coming into her mouth—and spring—are (in one) without any authority motivating them, there. Authority of any kind, one's creating, must be grasped and removed from anything.

Her particular instance of family authority is and has to be in the future foreseen as connected to people wading in rose-black sewage in the streets whose sewage-lines were to be restored by Halliburton, the US company that skims the cream of graft in Baghdad from the US government, for them and the US leaders who hold shares of Halliburton, the graft occurring as open intention on the US part unknown to us. There isn't authority in either—that is, not in any single of a pair, (of authority behind this, which is in her, isn't seen yet by her), or in (as) the two held together (any authority or basis, and that held in her), which would be imagination in respect to the sight she's to see of people wading in the sewage of their streets in spring now. Reads about it in the newspapers. Her being (person) is the particular authority that is in both of these small and large (a family and the outside terrain) instances *at once*.

This does not mean there is not to be authority in the sense of: not restoring the sewage lines to clean use. There must be that. But no authority behind or after any, even at once *while* restoring the sewage system. Because there is the open fur door.

For this reason, one has to find authority linked and noticed in oneself in space that is to unrelated outside events. Dismantle this activity. As it *is*. In the outside, but not stemming in any way from one's family, as it does *not* stem from that.

In that sense the people wading in the rose-black sewage in the streets—there, the sewage-lines that are thought by our people, told this, to be being or to have been repaired—are thought first at this second.

Or a rose is thought first (not the rose-black sewage burst). Or the sewage *is* thought first.

The people wading in it are thought first. So the two coincide, both are thought first—before any other is this second.

Now.

This doesn't help them, Laura observes. Right. (That is, no, it doesn't.) Though we're not at this second.

When it comes to it, the other remembers that the father whom she'd thought was exactly the same as herself, a misperception that is a thorough illusion now, seen years earlier when she was at a young age, had been doing the same thing as now: In the intention to be 'even-handed' between the three daughters, he would erase her completely by her characteristics not being spoken of there as none of the qualities were *allowed* mention by him or them. Meaning, to observe by speaking of it would be unfair to the others. This is not on her part, it was strange on theirs.

This has nothing to do with authority in the outside, since she did not rely on this definition (of anything *from herself*). And the separation is part of their absorption.

Boat-Bodies

The problem is that the imagination is the way things are occurring. Or is *what's* occurring. In any case. Apparently this is obvious but she didn't know it until now.

142

It is only an illusion that men, except their father for the time of their looking at him, perhaps their father too, but except T, have turned and move by as boat-bodies of deer, or maybe the hopping owl rose off of C's belly.

The boat-bodies of deer who are the men move through, here and there, but they also begin to be distinguished as only seen that way. Now one/she sees she is a boat-body herself. It's a relief. She can rest, always. She thinks, for a minute.

It has nothing to do with C, C isn't around at the moment. That she turned one into a pooch, another into an owl floating on some emerald green dewy grass within the forest has no force. Anyway. Out ahead—boat-bodies are seen.

Though the man one knows, calm, kind—beside her the mysterious deer-body— floats walking, or at night lying in the dark between the red sun and the moon early— leaps over the enflamed brush everywhere when the forest catches fire.

It catches fire in winter, but he's very steady and clear, not cool dark crystal. While running, she sees a deer running appearing to be afire.

C's long slender legs curled around the waist of the quiet man or the violent man who's *then* a pooch or is *later* on the emerald hill only black at night. For it is childhood and elderly life at one time. For her. For both. There is never lack of memory. Of the senses, but how are events anywhere. Are animals who weren't people aware of making something else by their they're being together so everything is changed. Do they change everything so then it is different, or so events occur differently, far from them: from their being together. And can they know this. Star is a hill at night but is a war evening. Plants do change each of the instants: is *their* authority outside—events *then* are different from what we're seeing making.

The use of time. Episodes that occur—as these occur in their consecutive 'order' (is now). The mother had had an inner life. Life (hers) through her imagination. Last night walking rain.

What I saw when I was walking through the city beside a main thoroughfare, a blue heron dipping its legs as trays in the air floating low slowly, almost touching the person with its legs when floating over in day—through the neighborhoods—it went right next to (in space, both frontal) the memory of the little girl with the other little girl, come home from school, told by their grandmother their dog Jet died hit by a car that day. This is beside the blue heron floating over one. The little girl bursting into tears puts next to it And we paid so much money for it! from the Pound. Petals are time, of years—only on blossoms on trees. One day or one time, the two girls together remember the dog, and the girl who'd burst out We'd paid money for it!, said to the other You said then: And we paid so much money for it! reversing them in the horizontal space. Because time and space have been compressed by her. No, it was not I who said that, *you* did. Yes, it brought out the worst in me! now the girl remembers. Petals are time but also a mirror in which side-by-side one thing is the other throughout, for her. Not for someone else maybe. Or: this wouldn't happen to anyone else.

In war, we have the leisure to remember anything.

A train in space clacking overpass over the city, seen at once through both rows of windows on either side, jolting as it hurls is in space by a phone call (next to it in horizontal space though of eight years earlier than it) from the enraged little girl who pours out wrath that her mother having been asked by her to allow her (the daughter) to arrange the mother's things before her death, sort through her things before she died—that was eight years before she died—has refused. One asks the-con-sumed-with-wrath You said *that* in relation to her later death. There are no questions since the president has blinded us—so the wrathful is alerted to one hearing her. In a few days, the mother, who would not usually speak of another in the family to another, this time mentions, and almost weeps that she's been hurt by (the little girl) having asked to sort through her things before her death. An aside from one to Iago who fishes a few days later—finally leads one to say this event to Iago. And Iago says immediately She didn't say this! (the little girl didn't say she'd wanted to sort through the mother's things). But how could I know it if she hadn't said it—She called *me* (who was hearing) and said it—I'm saying it *after!* No: she *didn't say* it! Iago says on the phone, long distance. Wrathful here is then in rational actions. She's realigned. By herself and, at once, by someone else elsewhere. There meets a black butterfly that skims ahead wobbling and making the air. She *makes* everything. It is different from an inner life, there there is none.

Men who were supplicants to C. But the question is Why are only they changed. What is oneself—A boat-body too. You've been holding yourself in abeyance, separate in living not just in not dying yet. Concentrating on one thing separately. But one moves.

Others were hardly given time or attention (though they might not notice) to say a word while wrathful who seems jolly there talked in her deprivation uninterrupted in a loop without listening. To anyone. Any speaking would be omitted. Omitted that was outside, considered boring. Nothing returned (in the jolly one's [wrathful's] speaking), didn't speak of or admit the outside into the loop, sometimes speaking at the same time as others. Eventually, next to them all is a mesh that's a black butterfly that is rational action, unspoken. That is, speaking is being led by someone else—the butterfly is doing a rational act that is the same thing or instance there (the same as: that no one is allowed, by everyone, to speak except that one absorbing).

Two things begin to meet in the space. That itself. It is 'the' space, meaning 'anything there'—horizontal includes and subsumes vertical.

What's revealed is that one can think anything. 'Concentrate on something else' is a tautology. That's what people are.

One cannot unravel a loop—there's nothing to unravel. It never touches itself.

It's also a tsunami wave reversed *in* to one and people. Because there are so many people.

Blank, oneself not identifying it, has been mystified by pop garbage spewed into other people, such as from talk shows. That were going on all this time, while she never watches television. But this phenomena is not tsunami wave, though it isn't surface either, in altering people. Their *behavior* is a tsunami wave.

A tsunami wave is people's behavior, which is also their speaking or thought [I'd thought], it has to have been *done*—has to be acted on space. Crowd running. Speaking to. After. After what.

Of course there aren't any rational actions.

Second is going to concentrate on something simple. One as a boat-body is submerged—but also loves (because one does) though one's eyes just see.

Still, a body is a jellyfish, a colored cape pumping in-place with no bone in it. They think.

While the boat-body is a deer banging in the forest with as against its sides, there is a part of one that doesn't have bone. Also the jellyfish pumps its cape held in the illumined there. The same body. But the deer anyway has an aspect that is boneless, humped flying with the legs drawn up to leap jumping over a bush, the moon standing on its one edge there. Before the deer, before its boat-body.

The soldiers are throwing the bodies into the Euphrates

River she comes in says by mouth after hearing

it
the streets are choked stacked with the people
's corpses

.in that they won't allow people to leave the US soldiers

are throwing the bodies into the Euphrates

the US
to conceal the numbers

dead

saying only insurgents are killed. but more

than a 100,000 people

remained in Fallujah when before

the fighting

started starts

the president of Iraq says anyone there still is an

insurgent

the event wasn't spoken   *as occurrence*

no civilians

there   fore   arc killed
                                 in the event

the difference and the relation between saying by mouth

                                                        and
the (written phrase)
also event not spoken *as occurrence*   is
                                                        in space
they   come
                                                        out

In this shape in space, or during it 'being'—after it—the Second's mother passed
away (in this instant of falling asleep, now, remembering this burial had already hap-
pened, so she *must* have). The words "passed away" rather than "died" seem to now
(after her 'going,' 'not being here') mean something, the words appear not to be
euphemism. But there's no relation except in that space (a band or layer and time)
between the people in Fallujah and the one's elderly mother, apart from them 'going'
then nor were all the people killed there by fighting. The US soldiers demolished the
walls in the Fallujah citizens' space with them there. They were there in it. It wasn't
spoken *(as occurrence)*. Nor was the mother speaking (at the last).

The young woman coming in speaking this, the phrasing itself imitated an event in
space. The words were a stream in a shape that had come out of her mouth. They
were a structure in space in the room taking place in front of her mouth but every-
where and perceived by a hearer only. Second became a hearer also, in addition to
seeing, things other, elsewhere.

Only what one doesn't know happens. May include mirror image reverse: Use of oth-
ers only then they bound there. One does also. Abandoning of the center occurs from
the people. The view that the father had abandoned one is altered by him. We speak.
He had attempted throughout to move the others without abandoning them either.
They the others besides him don't move in her seeing. She is terrified by death now.

                    One's a wall to them bound

            off of it   to them   there isn't day death doesn't exist

there both 'our'   *only* existing

(his) love is one isn't a wall then or rose desert's walls

                                                        's walking one's

wall's 'walking' 'one's' 'wind' 'dusk' 'dusks'

Rule

A depression is a depression in space and it has

                                                        no

                                        equivalent

in authority

Depressed dusk walking. Rain is dusk *as occurrence then.* One isn't event, except *as occurrence.* Though speaking wasn't *that* event *as occurrence* ever.

                        They're coming to check-posts, if they

                                                do not respond

                to the hand-signals   to slow

        or to firing in the air   by the US soldiers
        who say   they'd signaled
        the Italian journalist kidnapped returned by the
                                                        insurgents

                        they're being shot

                                                        first

returned is shot speeding toward a check-post, the

                                        agent

in the car with her   who'd

freed her from the insurgents   is killed

                all from this a train

by the US soldiers   bombs go off in the roads

everywhere

        black rose-sewage train   beside them

and night   everyday killing

civilians   and US soldiers

                                who say any

words after   first
        a family of five coming to the check-post is
                        day is beside them too at once
fired on the parents are killed   the newspapers say

the children were covered in the parents' blood they

live—a man deported from the US to Syria so

                                they

                                can

                                torture him

        push outside him

unlike the US   the relation to deportation
is
bursts of blossoming trees here   not in
                      black rose-sewage grounds

says everyday they beat him yet the Syrians say

                      he's no connection   to

                                              terrorists

now, is not related   after they

                                         tortured him

it's upheld in the US 'we'   *can*

                                    deport

people who'll   be tortured to be tortured *there* on

one side   is day   and a   night
on the other side   there is   horizontal
                                           here

this, on the level of black rose-sewage,

                                        hasn't authority
in order   that
not cycle   every event of any sort
                                        be first

This intrinsically, on the level of black rose-sewage, hasn't authority. But on other levels it does.

A dumb thought, which there aren't. Thoughts. But one has to flatten space in order that every event of any sort (eventually here) be first.

Depressed dusk walking—rain dusk walking alleviates death (of a mother—who not being there, the effect of that) slightly—the light and dark dusk is everywhere soft in pouring dusk rain—the buildings there that are also the vertically falling rain shafts, in them/the buildings, which they are (rain), and trees boughs in the dusk *are* the heavy rain first.

                    Precedes as rule with everybody dying a wave of every
                    thing dying yet first and   now mature

                    lovely woman major in the Marines   who's

                    Hawaiian   and lost

                                                                      both

                    her legs   a pilot of a helicopter that was blown

                                                                      up in

                    Iraq
                    testifying to
                    a committee on the needs of her soldiers   her losing

                    both legs

                    having happened right before the committee   one
                    is to have to not be in either family or the outside
                    not   from one's choice but
                    by events'   occurrences   only

                    both my choice and the events are the first occurrence
                              others are first there her   and

                    floating above the people is the blossoming roof here
                                                                 only once

                    _____

At once Halliburton recipient of the US govt

contracts to

                          rebuild the bombed   and

wrecked Iraq   is paid ten billion, in that the

US vice president has shares in the company, over
charged by a hundred million for work not performed

          while *their* streets swim in   black

                                  rose-sewage

       a split in one and blossoming trees

their civilians are arrested and removed   *on*

no charges   horizontal   to quell

discontent—while the contractors are not arrested

yet one is neither in the family nor in the outside why

does one see one is no longer in   the

                                  outside
anywhere   *our*

actions   bound
. so the city swims above and in the midst of it the

blossoming plum trees
have to not be in either, not in the outside at all oar
or a family

their   occurrences are

so her choice and the events beside it are both first

                                           there rose

_____

A
m not either in the family or in the outside why
does she (I) see she is no longer in the

is there   outside by

beside huge numbers peoples surface   cruising

                                        on

                                     the floor

of the rose desert is broken floating

                                     one's

the enflamed iris pushes out on   blossom

                                   ing trees roof
         everywhere   rose

surface   makes a hole in space's

air   from their

     the old as rule the forest is in the Euphrates
                                 River
Toyota cruisers river falcon enters space of fore

stalling people dying   silent

                  words   first
so, not   from it
plane there whose planes are invisible to birds

colliding with them   where birds

                                       can *see*

the falcon   where is the surface of the rose
                                 floor everywhere
drones floating killing the insurgents citizens
speaking separate   isn't

(the insurgents' speaking isn't)   first

nor is speaking the event's   *as occurrence*

these   (at) once

----

is everything only lying   separate
words
one
lies 'night' also   of someone else everyone

(why is)

dawn
the forest is in the Euphrates River

where
meeting the dead   occurs

only   asleep, in one
(words) in everyone   harmonious

do 'occur' in present wild friends here
are their words also   once

in that they're (one's)   *as occurrence*

events   bound   'night'
only (separate) outside   yet no one is

one isn't event, except *as occurrence*

in the outside (either)   can't *be*   places

one's mind by from first beside any streams of is

them once one's outside's

events rose desert is everywhere in
that peoples cruising their Toyotas on

the huge floor

break its surface
black rose day first one

Avril

People cruising

Toyotas the rose desert   breaks

everywhere   because they are on its surface then

only
a woman ignorant and from eyes blank gloating savaging
others   speaking only   no one speaks there they're

not reflected in her eyes her

either for her anywhere

tyranny of inverted in her/gloater's being defined as the
social outside

their kindness   a train hurls on tiers seen in the sky

no sight admitted
into the gloating one savaging others then doesn't make

sights   cattle came to a blossom

in others

so a man threw a ball

blank to everyone is inverted by her savaging speaking

only they cruise the
rose train surface

at
night

no reflection of anything on the rose floor everywhere

                             they leave the side

                    _____

Authority or abandoning had to have been before
As in the middle   midst
            so (one) is not outside either first
its/their weight is on (in) horizontal night as day also in

that   place 'trees' 'words'

                    a man regards people as only to serve
                                             him
sees nothing but matter   anyone   at the
requirement of someone else on the condition of *their*

                              slav   ery
to him   people given up are not slaves then
                                             offed
abandoned
                                             they

are set loose   black smoke comes out of a woman's
mouth   their black flowers there

                the soldiers walk

authority had to have been (before in one)   so (one)
                              is not outside either first
the roads to   see
      bombs hidden on the roads, a walking soldier may

be   blown in a road they make

the   invaded the living citizens arrested shot

                                        coming to the soldiers
                                              only driving
thin armor chicken-winged holding   it on
the soldiers' arms to their sides

                                        at the side of night loose
everywhere
                        there is no weight in or on it 'actually'

(it's only)   in occurrence (one's)
so they have 'imagined' 'one' is not there

after or first   no one   outside either
everywhere so   the 'flat' being of plants rose
trees   without their blooming   without

it bloom
she   a man who's kind a man threw a ball leaves

                                              the side

——————————————————

From the inside everything is matter   walking

                                             night
rose   word
'he'   re orders retroactively in having seen

                                         others
only (?) to serve him existing economically there
everything

is no side   at the side

of   night   rose   leaves

the separation,
which is joy   everything
there first   to others,

unseen retroactively

          there   (his)

night   rose   leaves

ahead   (of people)
no one so one not in the outside either while

                                   there

                           while it is there

———————————————————

As has to
be before crickets seethe sing are being the emerald hills that are

                                        a dark blue

                                                    day
no cobalt night can be there their singing at once is the emerald

                                            hill alongside a dark blue
                                            day only one

's seeing its (seeing's) occurring at all is before it's pink clover

                                                        sea

                that authority only abandons and offs would have
to have been that authority's occurrence, (night isn't) the con
                            dition of slavery, *before*

is one
defined from that authority, both, seeing the definition of outside
                                                    and not

                    the people fan out cruising   the rose
                                                    desert

            is not reflected in the pink clover sea on 'a' emerald sound
                                                    hills

            their having hearing is the social and 'night' cruising

                                                    the floor
there   see and sea dawn   it's a sea
                        breaks stars them anyone can speak a man

                                                    threw
a ball

                    _____

One's a wall to them bound

off of it to them   there isn't day death doesn't exist

there both 'our'   *only* existing

(his) love is one isn't a wall then or rose desert's walls

                                        's walking one's

that one is from language not in/from phenomenal night
                                              ever that
(night) and

        their our there language *is* death in that 'our' having
made   that everything here stars

words a man says "expressivity" is forbidden by him in
people   so he parts everyone   in their/its abaxial

leaf   separating is by beside his rules   regard
less of what every one any thing *is*   or from
                                                  soldiers rule

                                                  run

                                                  being
killed in (their they're) from phenomenal night *then*

only   he isn't yet

                        Alan saying Beckett's
"just personal" is by his figure's *being* an   Everyman

is it we're repeats every where people are thought

by Beckett to be mass that's of individuals   only

                                        not as

161

if
they created side together 'one' being invisible then

oddly in   rose mud sole
                                                        the
other man's "no expressivist" anywhere is neither 'night'
nor   theirs

                            that *'we're'* hasn't dawn

                                                wall of
            rose walking
abattage suborbital eye one's theirs began outside the future

        one's both   are outside one's suborbital eye   the

    future itself separately is the present here is endless

the same action outside then   cyclists in black coming *to*

                                            one for

                                        ward in streams

        ride by one after another to one on light day air they
                        jut black holes in its air

                outside sole on suborbital eye rose desert rushes
                                            to

                                            trees
        boats cycles horses bow in green that's
                                    their there
                cyclists ride bejeweled green on beside it every

                                        where
                        jewel flowers strew that

    outside green on flock of cyclists race there

_____

Ex in cite ment of get ting up be fore dawn to be gin wh

                                                    at to
                                    be gin a gain dawn

        be gins from night, no   or oar   be gins from that day
                                    be fore it one night comes

                                                for ward
        birds sing ing are hid den   fly ing by fly ing—we speak to

        them the trees height waves e ve ry where yet the cars
        cruise the   rose

        dawn be gin then two glis ten ing ly Ca na da Geese stood
                                                on the cliff of
        o cean th eyre honk ing on the o thers to come yet la ter
                                                they come in
        on   the men and wo men laugh ed
                the air eir honk ing ar riv ing oar in honk ing in
tan
                dem *makes* eir fly ing see ing two days

    the trees' si lence is sides thoughts edge
    one's not in either the outside   or oar
    rain pour s on red rose s and   a ny thing can't hear
    plants si lence are   theirs

    of the senses,   but how are events anywhere
    eir in re verse is for ward if we don't make the out side
                    drops out
    if *we're* not   the outside oar a gain

    are peo ple mass of in di vi du als then not mak ing that

    la ter to ge ther for   then out side sole

    first we're making *anything* 'ahead' future is itself and

    separately in 'the present here is endless' do they and

                              do the birds make or are the
                    out side s green on flock of cyclists race there

oar alter and make every thing out the side   *both*

                                     birds do ing so that

              they jut in black air beside there their the oar

out side that's blue

DeLay Rose

Occurrence of one's is without one once

        at once   two people

      in conversation—in outside's motion
                 as Creeley thought
                        words
    and speaking
                 as catching up to being in
                 that motion outside
                      (at) once

                 DeLay corrupts   to
money launder   falling out of

    intimidate lobbies so they're only being   on

one side while government rule is tied to favors on both sides of
floatation for their huge corporations' con   tracting and

officials on the take when they know nothing en events acting

one sun and moon at once by each other day at night *then* and
wrecked Iraq   Occur's first   with dome floating our penned
                      starving moved

also then   'our'

      president'd   for photos kiss the green corpses swim

     ing in the flood   than the living   transported in

outside's motion—the occurrence between—as Creeley thought

                        words

one's to catch up to being (in) one's events   at all? I

'd wake at night having dropped out of being in that event *then*
hav having terror that having to be in one's events and *not* being

in them then *when that*—is that like his in which   occur's *first*

                                where? one is first too/two not
                                caused anywhere they're only once/
                                            at once
outside of occurrence is_____? not.   Occur's first
                                is therefore also two—he'd
have
sentiments be actions, outside's motion *there* too. To occur first
                                is outside's motion
                                          of one

In Memory of Robert Creeley

———————————

DeLay's corrupt   decussation between the outside

and one still aleatory mazarine elands run

viewed

as on, that is, single line that's

an isobath   imaginary line   throughout flooded cities in the oce

ans   the govt's DeLay's Atlantis
waves everything's   one

's outside   the mazarine elands are two too a
                                hierarchy has to be more than one

man speaking of one man/hierarchy as acting on an ecstatic

single basis (words)   speaks as if no one else knows of that

or had (known) ever   Is an ecstatic basis as one's young only

when young? (by this time that one's dead) a basis isn't caused

                            outside isn't caused
there US soldier said they're told to kill prisoners rather

than

return with them to base, slaughtered them until Fallujah filled

with

numbers are transported   corpses

floated soldier says naked Iraqi corpses tied as a deer on a Hum

                            vee's hood,
sport   *Occur's first*   a corpse killed driven on the hood through

the streets dome floating ours penned starving moved—The

worst thing is—of the flooded poor here, left corpses swimming

—some of these people (will) want to *stay* in Texas, as if they

already do will want, the mother

of 'our' president says who's from Texas.   penned have

been   transported

from the flood   crowd not on isobath   each
enters by speaking it

Set at a certain place is or comes in only *there* at our sides so

blae sky our rubble on isobath float one drops any line; that is,

also   in one that one line so there could be anything occurring
there   ocean   together (without it)

a split in being one and that's being in language also words are

occur's first   ec

static two

Are things a being in ecstasy are first together—not caused there

one's here split between day and night is a
one's structure *for*/to be its it's anti-structure being outside only

one no longer able to catch up to one   separated   a delay

for roses first on a roar

———————————

                                              Occur's first

the mazarine elands are two heard the split between day and

                                                        night

one's (my) having the split in one—so ecstatic basis single is not

                                                      caused

there—soldiers are still and run   there's no isobath as line in o

                                                      ceans

                                                      begin

                          _____

DeLay rose and

the flower (rose) yet it's action only outward not vertical or
there   our soldiers do horizontal night raids

                    kick the doors down and line up the inhabi

                    tants battalions patrol a crowd of young Iraqis

                                                                taunt

                    ing them then a rocket-propelled grenade fired

                                                        from "insurgents"

sailing into the chest of the driver, Staff Sgt. Dale Panchot it
nearly cut him in half   the death of Panchot changed

                                                        them for the

                            battalion wrapped the town

                    in barbed wire giving the men in it identity cards in

                    it's action that isn't split or

English only   if you have one of these, you can come and go, if

you   don't have one of these, you can't

                    before taking two men to the river   (can't's)
action isn't outward or horizontal   or

                    it was Venus, going away, striking her deconstructed

                                                        forehand
with conviction   mazarine elands run

                    with Venus, not her sister, rising

playing sister Serena in US tennis Open   action's
the gap between sleeping and not dreaming and dreaming and

                                                                    waking

both run the plop of the air borne ball from them with Venus's
        or from her   deconstructed forehand (a concept) first

                                        leading them   'our'
president's brother's just now, the middle, detached the poor

from   their

having medical care

        in a law that will lead to detaching them in this eve
rywhere in the country the poor when they're ill or dying will

be uncovered   corpses swim

in   the underwater city   leading

Be uncovered

                        ————————————

                                                    Containing
            the plomb is being   their/our speaking   (and) *not,*
in *their* hemming her,   ever matching their tones to be one as lo
                              wer there everywhere. so one con
structs *is* listening as this speaking to be   not doing *their*
                              this speaking which is only
their enforcing hemming   one and event   just by being born in
                              this have only this space
in the US, being is (one) out of one's skin yet having thought—is
                              the thought in skin that
            —'intestine's in one's eyelids'   *is* one's only occurre
                                                              nce
                                                              there
?   moon in space is not in time (with) 'when' one'll in forest
be 'on' speaking, one's to at every instant undo as being, come
                  up to, *as* (in) speaking almost just match and
                              at once sensation
just *not* 'match' their outside (construction) being hemmed there

            '*only* in this space' is same as actions, as 'not' in   'this' time
one's hearing is (in one's actions) doing away with speaking, any
                                                              then

            _____

                              Intestine's in eyelids
no habits one's a plomb of walking and seeing   *that*
                         Yet a person's   'living *to* die'
                                                          is

in and 'is'
forest of people killing and or their seeing that they're
(not) 'people's acceptance' is there at all the same as their being
there
                    also their intestines in their eyelids while
                                                     still living

                                                          One's

a plomb of walking and seeing stopped but as that walking and
                                                      seeing

plomb of corpses that swim at surface underwater
city's   not split between their decomposition and

                                             night

                                             either

Addington's having made legal   torture and imprisoning con
structing govt rule   that without detainee's trial or

(there's *no)* charges they're on the mere accusation of their terror

ism   he's (Addington's) chosen as an
architect of their being no law

                         for anyone as their choice lives *to* die

they   *may*

              dead to replace schools   do so
                         not split between their decomposition and

                                                        night? night
is   one's plomb of walking and seeing and they're

split between what's seen and   people's

'acceptance' as if that were the being (anywhere) but isn't anywh
                              ere a lived plain that isn't there

                                                              is

plomb of everyone's *there*   *at*/once for an instant   *all*

outside's the (everyone's) plomb of walking and seeing *also* the

circle   ec   static   and   terror of not seeing?

or even terror of not having that (terror of) as being

dead while *their* 'here' and (in) Addington's outside motion

is legally the physical tortured peoples there

                                                              so
cial 'acceptance' is an illusion that is then not there then *either*

the separation between   the
choice of being seeing one's illusion/'people's acceptance' lived

                                                    and their

'not split between their decomposition and night'   is

                                                    terror

'Really' the dead-loved float away   they don't float   aren't there

                                                    for one
is 'one's choice to live *to* die'   —in that forest is—

                                                outside outside?

                        ————————

176

                                        'Intestine's in eyelids'
                                              the line
outside

and —words/I thought—Creeley seeing that/my 'it's ours'—

'our' 'acceptance' people's 'to be accepted' one seeing and being

                        we're   that

and, lived by one, that isn't there even—*ever*—we're within

this then it's its constraint of their enforcing running ghouls'
            propriety—the propriety of ghouls—where there one

has/having to play   is. Creeley getting it that of one's seeing

                                              that

                                              the
one there from 'our' 'their ghouls'/they're *really doing that*
            dead to replace schools   do so

not just quadrumane, but forest of killing and also dying as 'to

                live *to* die' (in one's) ? being the
                                              same

are   outside of 'to be accepted' [the outside/social is people's

                acceptance only illusion lived nowhere

                                              else

than dying also their 'not split between their decomposition and
                                              night'

night *also* the plomb]   while having to play there,   is

            so as that, someone else mocks seeing   that at all

                                              177

even, mocking one seeing it, though another's mocking because
it's   one's,

                                                                   is this one's seeing? not
                                                                   his (Creeley's),
which they'd admire—*their hierarchy*—and Creeley *not*

making that *as seeing itself* (*not* making hierarchy sees)—while
                                                          they are (making theirs)

where   really outside playing   that's   any
one's   as   seeing   that's   only   also

            not split between their decomposition and night

the
stars and the moon (may) break the crust as *in* one's/their the
                                                                                     eyelids

                                ///

Not even in the brain   just is in   /is
                                              between the eyelids

                    _____

A man   leaves   the side

Chaka's   and stars run in day
(Chaka's)   a
whirling dervish there runs at 200 miles an hour where the wind
                                              's.
the sensation
              one's mind undoing and seeing *their* actions and
                                    one's in

              that are before, everywhere

events   waking (once) in night   *that*   it's night *also*

                                     separately there
(is) mine d that's lying-night there was the sense [after? mind *it's*

undoing events to order these—which *there* isn't?   the plomb (or
                  der) that stopping   see these (events)

    'is everything only lies?' even is irrelevant as is also some

one's saying *he's* dropped a unity, at all, and *one's* is just to have

a   whereas this is their sentiment also 'whole'   ness
is inaccurate, he says, which is not Grenier's his is wordless *with*
words
              mine d outside of my seeing my action of *that*
                               (ordering),
              outside or outside events
before or after mine d] (not) undoing night or in it is   (*'not'* is
a side in we're before these events   )

      once   stars 'unseen' 'at' and had 'sense' of well-being there

                  as a child anticipating *there*

being ahead every day in or there wonder of 'what's there?' of
                                    having

                                                                these
days ahead   'here' a day's in
the   inclement warm wind blasting fast huge red fall   leaves
        the side   seen outside roar

my ine not returning to these waking dur ing the a night and the
        sensation not having occurred before myself's a space

                    stopped night *that* once

                                                there events
                                                unfold outside

                        ———————————

Some (read *red/silent)* their touching down at night in Spain fuel
                                        ing planes on
        which are the secretly captured US transport ing prisoners
                                moving them to be tortured *by*

others for the US   outside where torturing's legal

                                and separately nothing but here

        the warm wind blasts ing fast huge red fall leaves the side

        a (some) woman's lying that is   sentiment (is
                                her 'emotion as lies') describes
herself emotion (says grief, anything) that's or 'will' (have)   cru
el ty /killing/overwhelming others/ (have as) greed
                                                transform
                                                s has

                                                everything

also   beginning there   is *one's* emotion's action   now

occurrence but it goes on before myself's a space also   past

'one' as in her (some) now having savaged outside and one in it
                                present but in this having

been him who's basis he 'let' her is being *in* her volatile actions*are*
oneself *(from them)*   become invisible

feel dying   a split that's their and actions' present removes
mine d they're not existing   the basis that

                                                                is
                                                even *there*
not ['not' is and 'night is plomb *for* the sensation of walking and

                        seeing'] existing one's outside every thing

isn't   other's behavior *here not*

determined or any *in* lying-night warm wind that Chaka's
in (Chaka's running)   in

                    at day huge red leaves

                                   day leaves

                                   the side

———————

                                                        and (before)

past-waking at night as *at* that (night) with the sense   (young)
of terror one not being (in) one's own action of that *then*   (wak

ing)   not caused   ec

stasy isn't an intent   *Occur's first*, before   where

peoples   transported in

out
side's motion—the occurrence between—I others thought/read

(red/silent) then *'at' that* night in their instants also outside being

in Addington's action   who's the architect to torture
here

                                                          now a
man says oneself *(then*/young) being adjusted 'would' see there
         's not terror   *or* adjusted then there's not
that   their subject terror

ism   now

is 'adjusting on an imaginary line in oce ans and one

separate from oneself not being in events yet *as* one *is in* them'

                                                          (then

                              is to catch up to being) *there,*

whereas that separation one sees later   as having been before
                                                          also
in one's every day and night one had made a line   *that's*

(theirs?) *night* is plomb *for* the sensation of walking and seeing,

the separation that's   then it *isn't* except walking and seeing
being in it   lying in night waking and seeing   (once hav

ing pre-jammed mine d   has well-being there (having) once or
                                   dered

      outside *as* it's one

---

it's one's early life or at all. now *in*
their volatile actions killing (one/relative s)   become invisible

a   who're one's   split that's their and action's present
                                                           removes
mine d

one's not existing   any   where   being/in it   pre
                                                                past

jammed mine d find   since they're erasing every one is   hav b
                      actions at all any aren't *in* one's *that are*
                                                         occurring

          being in it   lying in night-waking and   (once

) I'd 'one' mine the sensation of 'has' well-being there mine   d

not there as being at once outside *also?*   Now do it. yet I   *can't*
                                                     night is there

Were actions imaginary line dropped in one being actions by be
                                                             side
                                                             there?

——————————

Walking and seeing night the plomb one

's still not

changes it to meet it   *then*

'we' the plural as *with* the dead either   when (one's) existing in

'one's to catch up to being (outracing) *in* one's own actions, that

not split between their decomposition and night   one's in

then'   there behind. they're not. Creeley later broach
                                                            ing (e)d his

dropping even any imaginary line of his one's actions of   lying-

night   seeing this to b

e in these all every days that aren't one's ones

there only continually and ec

tasy not an intent day's not a line there is *also* that where occur's
                                                                      first

is

(is) that the same as one's 'intestine's in one's eyelids' all
                                                              the time

that motion outside   a man runs   'will' there's 'the next

day' 'at' the side   Chaka's   stars   run

s?

———————————

CAPITALS the line imaginary Oce ans *also* 'dropped there' in
(that are)this w
ay of 'there' being no separation (one's) between the day and the

night either

present where (is action) I

'd (before) dream hand(ed) the dream to someone else in it fin al

ly because mine d need ed (need)s to sleep yet b
al
ways a   wake (ing) in both all 'their' time isn't outside *there*

as one being awake in them   is only one's actions (of)   even dr

eaming this (that one is hand ing dream (ing) that to someone

else, in one *too*
) rather *'was'*   anything's   *'there'* at once

The instant I heard my own voice T says What? to it now though
I did*n't*
say anything had n't
he heard it (mine) too   people wonder   why do it? Chaka dream

s   running   cries   Chaka's being

chased dreaming   is seen by one outside outside Chaka   leaves

the side
's /one's (an action)   also
sur
veillance   Chaka's   to be in that languageless dream ing seen

isn't what's the

surveillance   bounds   (in) outside of

almost a year and hate has come up emerging as if not there b
                                                            efore
(is just there, when not volatile, *or is,* after their/others' action
                                                          omitted/

silent loved-dead) *in one* shown *from* these/they're left not hav

ing been seen   *in them*   ever

it's all il lu mine d wild pain   in that they'd deserted one too

deserted everyone? real-ly one made up living   too

outside Chaka

---

   b

                                                              efore

(silent loved-dead) *in one*   shown from *others*   having
                    in this not having been seen   deserting

                                              (there) *there*

                                              ALL CAPITALS

'S the next day's   *too*   a man says another's (an action)
          one's   ,not there,   in pain *from* their/*others* shown

DO ACTIONS DO ANYTHING AT ALL? IS ALMOST DREAM
                                              ED

        is mine d in day   'ec
stasy'   as if only one   other, in *that* man's hero worship had

        the now-dead   ever

had ecstasy, while it would have to be a state we're *in*   to be

                                                        oar
for
asylum-seekers Rumsfeld mak*es* it more difficult to emigrate *here*

'only' (except dreamed) 'at' the edges *where* young or   peoples

transported   *past*   a man   leaves   trees   looks   'at'   the   side   s

        'at'once while one speaks a woman always mock(s) ing any occu
rrence, so social   that's

                                              189

'ones' b
of any would b
e the split that's decomposition *before* or here alive/between e

vents *where* is *'then'*/space she's outside them (and)
one

_____

's 'the side s push ed don't reappear' but maybe they *will!/silent*

— hating (one's now) shown *from* them deserting one   *too's*

('s) their deserting the loved-dead by mine d's the physical being
                                                                                        and

on*e's*   imprisoned

day/dawn by near their who *'re* action the split seen by beside I

'd had   the view (of) *you* 're not born   *with anything*   to

move whereas you   *are*   *too* (!/silent), it turns out, seen is a

'the' round's the plomb meeting anything split actions (is)   we
're split *there* Chak*a's*

          leaper with *a* star   both once run *in* a star in many
                                        there the person mocking's
          imagining (at)   all the events sense also   is
                                                              hierarchy
at all   lo
                                              wer except her 'happy

in people's acceptance' which doesn't exist outside this it's e mo

tion 's negative extraordinary rendition (s) 's(silent)actions *there*
                                                              outside Chaka

———————

We*'re* just left
a   left

                                                                                        leg

            is mine d in (':'/silent) day
in night   'ec

crosses *'in'*/stasy'

            the day is in the night

the middle raining sheets of rain   'at' night   not

being *then* (those at that time) in day

            but/and one being there

            ———————————

Extraordinary rendition (s) to go *on*

———————————

The (one)   social   someone mocking's as

               if everything's separated
                    the only 'being in'

                              was   *is*

to be on an edge constantly that's description of

itself (her someone else's description) *as* (being) its subject not

                            existing

                      their hierarchy is b
                        e ahead of one

the small level of misuse and the large appear to mirror
each other, go on at once   as if that were causation

wondrous its subject being not existing could be 'outside
                      outside'
                 While slipped off,

that be comes *has* finally/now how or how

                     not to

do (theirs) there's description of *that* one's

                 future life

               theirs, not existing
               there wondrous
not-even (ing) or night-dawn or to jump out of that

          that's subjecting

          ——————

If they haven't 'aren't' 'love's truth,' as Creeley

        would (did) say, the phrase and they

                                    're

one's early late life are now hasn't isn't existing   one's

why b hurt   in that 'love's truth' is   *occur's first*

did   in one, in

             him, in a man one's *with* some in

             night/dawn even the side   div

             moved over   de(c i) (vi) de(d) ing

                 just(/single   ones) *here*

        ———————

Cross *es* Cha*ka's* own will races inatten
tion disinformation mine d is only moved-one as   there   is *by*

them man in/other's actions saying Forget! simply (to one) (and)
                                                                then one

                                    can't even exist

                                    he'd *made* this

beside *by* their/other's force the only existing is theirs-ones *(isn*
                                                        'n'/ is)
                                                    simply there
a   left

                                                        leg
just in
at wild night night being in it already is noticed
DeLay rose   unrelated to Syria-warned to accept international rule
                intwined

                    hemmed by US who 're tor tur ers' extraordinary rend
                                tion to *other* countries Egypt
                                                    tortures
                for the US as
the president ours says *We don't torture*   undermined Syria a
                cused of undermining including mur dering *can't*

                    itself   ,though we do,

            say Syria (one) needn't (won't) be ruled   why is Syria to be ru
                                                                led?
                        itself
                        'is everything only lies' destabilizing them/every thin

there when   destabiliz
                                                    ing is the inten
tion

at wild night night being in it already is noticed

to her lighting the whirl er's ing's lying there   Cha-k*a's* :

Chaka-knows-bees
Chaka-knows-bees-and bees-and bees
Chaka-knows
bees

sang ing's the moon clef and treble in signs to 'us'

Chaka-knows-bees-and bees-and bees

without my/one knowing *by*
that sound she 's identified *bees* our s *(their)* (are) actions outside
(that) *are* language in one (outside) *too*

both one *sees* *their* meeting in that of Chak a's *that* that

Chaka-knows-bees-and bees-and bees
at wild night day night being in it already is noticed

as
occur's first

crossed *es* her the whirl er's own *will*/action *(t)here/ outside*

is

The use of *italics* /*as are*

Birds *flew*   ,   all   ,   *are*   ,

(*their s as((=)*

                                                                                        outside

                                                        ///

A backlog that's a dismantling   of anything that

                                                                                        mak*es*

any kind of sense their/poor/care/place of living/change that's
                                                                hope and I keep try
ing to *dismantle it* in mine as if that's/already-dismantling's *any*
                                                                outside/ *future life*

here
(mine d   is sensations even) as only *as* one's living now, when
there isn't any

                                as there isn't,in decomposition,

to alter 'the' (as a) basis   'economic/and mine d'   both/*single*
('re defined as single)

                        _____

For
asylum-seekers Rumsfeld's makes it difficult to   emigrate

here

Mac Low's *sing ing?* in that the side s are there 's(/silent)

speaking *'s* (/ silent) in being sounded he leaves the side s   in

flected into 'there' of as event is night-chance-determined
there isn't even

at wild night day night being in it already is noticed in the e
vents

and *no*   obligation of_____*(that's theirs)* and obligation of

giving everything to that person (on

their part) simply
from one being born
at wild night day night being in it   and

asked what obligation US soldiers in Iraq *had*

if
they saw Iraqi security forces abusing prisoners   Gen

Pace says It

is

absolutely the responsibility of every US service member, if

they see   inhumane treatment being conducted,

to

intervene and stop it
it is

the responsibility of every US service member
if they see any of US forces abusing prisoners in Iraq   it's
their
there (/silent)
responsibility   to

intervene and stop it
is implied
there Rumsfeld intervenes if they saw see Iraqi security forces

abusing prisoners
every US service member should *(no)*

report ing's it only, it's implied *If*

they are *physically* present (?) when inhumane treatment *is*

taking place,
sir, they have an obligation to try to
stop it, intervene

s Gen Pace   (is)
there

Mac Low's phrases   's/silent Pace

says later There's no difference between their views as *his*

was speaking ('s) of the obligation of US soldiers in
war   whereas Rumsfeld's was

                              of US soldiers in nonhostile zones
   at wild night day night being in it *(too)*

                                                    before/there
                                                         ones

            In Memory of Jackson Mac Low

                    _____

Is mine d good for anything? when
someone else 's *see* what's in power however the bully
            is if cru el bullying-gluttony corrupting, if it's in *then*
he sees it as 'good'/he's got to *see*(ing) overwhelming mere
ly in *then* to be as apparently strength since it's there is 'good'

that (it) had been the/a basis , *any authority , (for him)* b hurt
by it/his?

            [italics are both]   that one *comes from*

            that *he'd* see (omitted) is my mine d actions if I
                 omit see inside by being exterior circle

                                                              there

extraordinary rendition 's to go *on*

                                   ///

            Mac Low said to me I don't believe in the 'inside'

                 'only' or 'when' *they 'r making both?*
                                 r/*both* side s/at once

            his
single syllables 's halo halos of an *exterior* circle which
                 (rather than our being in it 'circular')   (which)

            one hears *as* he's 'do ing' this the syllables *there?*

                                   and we're not *'in'* that

                            _____

A
pressed freighter a

black dawn isn't at the black's owl whooing is

imagination for Chaka running dreams
there
it is *for* black

For Michael McClure for Mysteriosos & Cameos

One wave arises and kills everywhere in the

tsunami floating 'here' on other waves

                                                     there are

tears of joy emitted at things 'Is everything only lies?' is

there Chaka flies at two hundred miles an hour in stars

                                               there   though

it's day, both   from cells the bully is in the/her

                                                        own

sight of her bullying and hurting others gloats but alter

                                                      ed in

her lies, the trapped floating hatred arises in one recepi
ent to wild hatred arises yet one may *(can't)* delay rose

                        reasonless bully   rose flowers

DeLay (lay/silent flowers) impedes arising   but altered

McClure's word 'reason' is outside clear one sees at once

                    a *the* moon with Venus   occur's first

                                                  star that being

                                                  s destroying

anyone
here
theirs are only lies 'people's acceptance' the butterflies

                                                      that

die ever freighter OF METAL is pressed on sky that's
                  a   tsunami

                                                   'wave'

                                                    Riding in jeeps
                                                    that run the dunes
peak one

                    on the huge Sahara waves dimpled fold the
instantly crescent   *sun*   though the full moon's also

                                                there hour our

                                                    only here
                    r no coincidences that are appearances as one's random e
                    vents but (is) here anywhere there's *only* coincidences

at all appre r close so not succession ec static   that
                wa
            ndering in the huge sienna red sand black not-construct
                            ed rock pillars crescent-jagged

        the crescent-jagged black huge buttes-pillars move *on*

        our dilated flat day and night (don't or do/to have)   *red*
                        sand   , one's in the same place as

outside that's not words work were we're do
                                                        while
black stars one's we're   crest
a they
call whoop to each other for the jeeps *to* run the crest of
        as 'yets go!'   one a
        to
dune we come up to each mountain where at once there
                                        ere crescent eclipsed

                                                sun

and any   acts
ours/both: 'both' 'they jet' *from*/and call *ing* whoop and

the jeeps run *to* peak one on the other waves .

GREEN INTEGER
Pataphysics and Pedantry

Douglas Messerli, *Publisher*

Essays, Manifestos, Statements, Speeches, Maxims,
Epistles, Diaristic Notes, Narratives, Natural Histories,
Poems, Plays, Performances, Ramblings, Revelations
and all such ephemera as may appear necessary
to bring society into a slight tremolo of confusion
and fright at least.

*

Individuals may order Green Integer titles through PayPal (www.Paypal.com).
Please pay the price listed below plus $2.00 for postage to Green Integer
through the PayPal system. You can also visit our site at www.greeninteger.com
If you have questions please feel free to e-mail the publisher at
info@greeninteger.com
Bookstores and libraries should order through our distributors:
USA and Canada: Consortium Book Sales and Distribution
1045 Westgate Drive, Suite 90, Saint Paul, Minnesota 55114-1065
United Kingdom and Europe: Turnaround Publisher Services
Unit 3, Olympia Trading Estate, Coburg Road, Wood Green,
London N22 6TZ UK

*

OUR TITLES [LISTED BY AUTHOR]

±Adonis *If Only the Sea Could Sleep: Love Poems* [1-931243-29-8] $11.95
Tereza Albues *Pedra Canga* [1-899295-70-9] $12.95
Will Alexander *Asia & Haiti* [Sun & Moon Press: 1-55713-189-9] $11.95
Pierre Alferi *Natural Gaits* [Sun & Moon Press: 1-55713-231-3] $10.95
Hans Christian Andersen *Travels* [1-55713-344-1] $12.95
Eleanor Antin [Yevegeny Antiov] *The Man Without a World: A Screenplay*
[1-892295-81-4] $10.95
Rae Armantrout *Made to Seem* [Sun & Moon Press: 1-55713-220-8] $9.95
Necromance [Sun & Moon Press: 1-55713-096-5] $8.95
The Pretext [1-892295-39-3] $9.95

Ascher/Straus *ABC Street* [1-892295-87-7] $10.95

Ece Ayhan *A Blind Cat Black and Orthodoxies* [Sun & Moon Press: 1-55713-102-3] $10.95

Ingeborg Bachmann *Last Living Words: The Ingeborg Bachmann Reader* [1-933382-12-0] $14.95

Letters to Felician [1-931243-16-6] $9.95

Krzysztof Kamil Baczyński *White Magic and Other Poems* 1-931243-81-6] $12.95

Djuna Barnes *The Antiphon* [1-899295-56-3] $12.95

Interviews [Sun & Moon Press: 0-940650-37-1] $12.95

Dennis Barone *The Returns* [Sun & Moon Press: 1-55713-184-8] $10.95

Martine Bellen *Tales of Murasaki and Other Poems* [Sun & Moon Press: 1-55713-378-6] $10.95

†Henri Bergson *Laughter: An Essay on the Meaning of the Comic* 1-899295-02-4] $11.95

Charles Bernstein *Republics of Reality: 1975-1995* [Sun & Moon Press: 1-55713-304-2] $14.95

Shadowtime [1-933382-00-7] $11.95

Régis Bonvicino *Sky-Eclipse: Selected Poems* [1-892295-34-2 $9.95

Robert Bresson *Notes on the Cinematographer* [1-55713-365-4] $8.95

André Breton *Arcanum 17* [1-931243-27-1] $12.95

Earthlight [1-931243-27-1] $12.95

Lee Breuer *La Divina Caricatura* [1-931243-39-5] $14.95

Luis Buñuel *The Exterminating Angel* [1-931243-36-0] $11.95

Olivier Cadiot *Art Poetic'* [1-892295-22-9] $12.95

Francis Carco *Streetcorners: Prose Poems of the Demi-Monde* [1-931243-63-8] $12.95

Paul Celan *+Lightduress* [1-931243-75-1] $12.95

Romanian Poems [1-892295-41-4] $10.95

Threadsuns [1-931245-74-3] $12.95

Louis-Ferdinand Céline *Ballets without Music, without Dancers, without Anything* [1-892295-06-8] $10.95

The Church: A Comedy in Five Acts [1-892295-78-4] $13.95

Andrée Chedid *Fugitive Suns: Selected Poetry* [1-892295-25-3] $11.95

Anton Chekhov *A Tragic Man Despite Himself: The Complete Short Plays* [1-931243-17-4] $24.95

Chen I-Chih *The Mysterious Hualien* [1-931243-14-x] $9.95

Dominic Cheung [Chang Ts'o] *Drifting* [1-892295-71-7] $9.95

Marcel Cohen *Mirrors* [1-55713-313-1] $12.95

Joseph Conrad *Heart of Darkness* [1-892295-49-0] $10.95

Clark Coolidge *The Crystal Text* [Sun & Moon Press: 1-55713-230-5] $11.95

Charles Dickens *A Christmas Carol* [1-931243-18-2] $8.95

Mohammed Dib *L.A. Trip: A Novel in Verse* [1-931243-54-9] $11.95

Michael Disend *Stomping the Goyim* [1-9312243-10-7] $12.95

Jean Donnelly *Anthem* [Sun & Moon Press: 1-55713-405-7] $11.95

±José Donoso *Hell Has No Limits* [1-892295-14-8] $10.95

Arkadii Dragomoschenko *Xenia* [Sun & Moon Press: 1-55713-107-4]
$12.95

Oswald Egger *Room of Rumor: Tunings* [1-931243-66-2] $9.95

Larry Eigner *readiness / enough / depends / on* [1-892295-53-9] $12.95

Sam Eisenstein *Cosmic Cow* [1-931243-45-x] $16.95
Rectification of Eros [1-892295-37-7] $10.95

Andreas Embiricos *Amour Amour* [1-931243-26-3] $11.95

Raymond Federman *Smiles on Washington Square* [Sun & Moon Press:
1-55713-181-3] $10.95
The Twofold Vibration [1-892295-29-6] $11.95

Carlos Felipe [with Julio Matas and Virgilio Piñera] *Three Masterpieces of
Cuban Drama* [1-892295-66-0] $12.95

Robert Fitterman *Metropolis 1-15* [Sun & Moon Press: 1-55713-391-3] $11.95

Ford Madox Ford *The Good Soldier* [1931243-62-x] $10.95

Maria Irene Fornes *Abingdon Square* [1-892295-64-4] $9.95

Jean Frémon •*Island of the Dead* [1-931243-31-x] $12.95

Sigmund Freud [with Wilhelm Jensen] *Gradiva* and *Delusion and Dream
in Wilhelm Jensen's* Gradiva [1-892295-89-x] $13.95

Federico García Lorca *Suites* 1-892295-61-x] $12.95

Armand Gatti *Two Plays: The 7 Possibilities for Train 713 Departing from
Auschwitz and Public Song Before Two Electric Chairs*
[1-9312433-28-x] $14.95

Dieter M. Gräf *Tousled Beauty* [1-933382-01-5] $11.95

Elana Greenfield *Damascus Gate: Short Hallucinations* [1-931243-49-2] $10.95

Jean Grenier *Islands: Lyrical Essays* [1-892295-95-4] $12.95

Barbara Guest *The Confetti Trees* [Sun & Moon Press: 1-55713-390-5] $10.95

Hervé Guibert *Ghost Image* [1-892295-05-9] $10.95

Hagiwara Sakutarō *Howling at the Moon: Poems and Prose*
[1-931243-01-8] $11.95

Joshua Haigh [Douglas Messerli] *Letters from Hanusse* [1-892295-30-x] $12.95

†Knut Hamsun *The Last Joy* [1-931243-19-0] $12.95
On Overgrown Paths [1-892295-10-5] $12.95
A Wanderer Plays on Muted Strings [1-893395-73-3] $10.95

Marianne Hauser *Me & My Mom* [Sun & Moon Press: 1-55713-175-9] $9.95